To Krista,
I thank God daily
that he gave me a
"low maintenance" wife like you.

Here's to fresh coffee, laughter,
sweet peas, and watching our children
grow together.
I love you.

D0063202

I Love You
unconditionally...

on ONE
condition

a2=1
BOOK

I Love You
unconditionally...
on ONE
condition

Everyday Choices for an
Extraordinary Marriage

JOEY O'CONNOR

Fleming H. Revell
A Division of Baker Book House Co
Grand Rapids, Michigan 49516

Published by Fleming H. Revell
a division of Baker Book House Company
P.O. Box 6287, Grand Rapids, MI 49516-6287
www.bakerbooks.com

Printed in the United States of America

Library of Congress Cataloging-in-Publication Data
O'Connor, Joey, 1964-
    I love you unconditionally, on one condition / Joey O'Connor.
        p.   cm.
    Includes bibliographical references.
    ISBN 0-8007-5902-8 (pbk.)
    1. Spouses—Religious life. 2. Marriage—Religious aspects—Christianity.
I. Title.
BV4596.M3038 2004
248.8′44—dc22   2003023333

Contents

Acknowledgments

The writing life is often a very solitary and challenging experience, as one flips on the computer and faces a blank screen for the day. Fortunately, I am surrounded by friends, mentors, and coworkers who encourage me along the way. I'd first like to thank my friend, brother in Christ, and literary agent, Tom Thompson, for his overwhelming enthusiasm and belief in me in championing this book. Tom's creativity, wisdom, and experience, along with keen insights, helped give pivotal shape and structure to this manuscript. It is a privilege to work alongside a friend and brother who keeps me focused on writing by taking care of the business details.

To my wife, Krista, and our four children—Janae, Ellie, Joseph, and Aidan—for their patience with me when I write on Saturday mornings and for the constant source of joy they provide. My life has been immeasurably blessed from being able to write at home and watch my kids grow up in the process.

To my father and mother, Joe and Jane O'Connor, whose lives and marriage are a constant source of inspiration; and to my in-laws, Herman and Donna Ahlers and Milo and Betty Lystne, for their support, friendship, and love to me and my family throughout the years.

To Milan Yerkovich, my mentor and friend, who has come alongside my life the past couple years and has made me a better man because of his wise counsel and discernment.

To Scott Hadley, Todd Dean, Glen Davis, and Mark Perez, four brothers and friends who have listened, supported, and prayed for me through many challenging seasons and transitions. They have shown me God's unconditional love and acceptance, which serves to remind me that God isn't finished with me yet. Thanks for pushing me along in the final six weeks of this manuscript when I was exhausted and felt like I couldn't type another word.

Last, this book would not be in readers' hands without the remarkable efforts of the Fleming H. Revell publishing team. I want to sincerely thank Jennifer Leep, my editor and personal champion at Revell, for her willingness to dream big and explore creative options and for the enthusiasm she brings to this 2=1 series. Jennifer, you are a pleasure to work with, and I appreciate all that you do on my behalf. A special thanks to Kristin Kornoelje for an excellent job editing this manuscript and making key suggestions for its structure. Books do not get to market without the creativity and persistence of people like Twila Bennett, Ruth Waybrant, and Karen Steele, who all lead the marketing and publicity efforts. Thank you for the personal attention and hard work you each brought to this book. Last, I want to thank the whole staff at Baker Books for their commitment to excellence and desire to see the body of Christ encouraged and inspired to bring the transforming message of God's unconditional love to the world.

Introduction

Walter Mittys with Everest dreams need to keep in mind that
when things go wrong up in the Death Zone—and sooner or
later they always do—the strongest guides in the world may
be powerless to save their clients' lives.

Jon Krakauer, Into Thin Air

I n early May of 1996, a little before midnight, two mountain
expedition teams left from Camp Four on the South Col
of Mount Everest in a bid to summit the world's highest
peak. Led by experienced professional Everest climbers Rob
Hall and Scott Fischer, the paying clients and Nepalese Sherpas
ventured out of their tents in subzero temperatures to ascend
the mountain the Tibetan people call "Chomolungma." Weather
conditions seemingly in their favor, team members strapped
oxygen masks on their faces and started up Everest's famed
Southeast Ridge, aiming at the 29,028-foot pinnacle looming
high above. A third group from Taiwan joined the conga line
inching up the mountain for what was to be a very long day.

No one could have foreseen the deadly combination of factors that led to the greatest tragedy in Everest history.

In his riveting work *Into Thin Air,* Jon Krakauer, a climbing journalist and client of Scott Fischer, offers a haunting account of the journey on Everest that fateful day. Three dozen people made the trip, most of them novice climbing clients paying upward to sixty-five thousand dollars and two months of their time for the privilege of being one of the elite few who have reached the peak. After coming so far, they were not about to back down.

The conditions on Everest are always hazardous. Above the "Death Zone" at twenty-five thousand feet, millions of brain cells are killed as climbers exert tremendous amounts of physical and emotional energy navigating their way up the rock and ice. Breathing is worse than trying to suck a lung's worth of air through a thin cocktail straw. And without adequate amounts of bottled oxygen, each climber is at risk of pulmonary and cerebral edema. Nail-pounding headaches throb. Vision becomes blurred. Senses dull. Objectivity and clear thinking diminish as consciousness falters. No matter how magnificent the view from the top of the world, life cannot be sustained in the thin air of a lifetime achievement.

By 1:00 P.M., the nonnegotiable turnaround time for Krakauer's group, several people including Krakauer had reached the summit and were in the process of making their way down. Among experienced Everest climbers, it is common knowledge that whether one has reached the summit or not, it is critically important to head down the mountain no later than the agreed-upon turnaround time to avoid being trapped high on the peak overnight, risking exposure to subzero temperatures, wind

> No matter how magnificent the view from the top of the world, life cannot be sustained in the thin air of a lifetime achievement.

and snowstorms, and the body's inability to sustain itself in such extreme conditions.

Earlier in the day, the congestion of so many people snaking their way up the mountain complicated communication and previously agreed-upon responsibilities. Anchors weren't set. Ropes went unfixed, wasting valuable time. The three expeditions became intermixed at various points up and down the Southeast Ridge. Hall and Fischer, along with other Sherpas, climbed with slower clients, trying to get them to the top, losing track of where their other clients were on the mountain. Once the turnaround time was ignored, everything necessary for a successful summit bid and speedy climb down went sideways.

With climbers now racing to get down the mountain and others still pushing for the summit, bottlenecks ensued. By 1:17 P.M., the wind picked up as weather conditions worsened on nearby peaks. As Krakauer snapped a few photos from the roof of the world, he saw in the distance what should have hastened everyone off the peak. "Training my lens on a pair of climbers approaching the summit, I saw something that until that moment had escaped my attention. To the south, where the sky had been perfectly clear just an hour earlier, a blanket of clouds hid Pumori, Ama Dablam, and the lesser peaks surrounding Everest."

Errors in communication increased as bottled oxygen reserves decreased. Altitude sickness drained logical reasoning. The climbers were extremely fatigued; most had not slept for the previous seventy-two hours. The resulting exhaustion slowed the group down as the stronger climbers literally dragged the weaker ones up and down the route. Poor leadership and bad decision making proved fatal.

By the time Krakauer made it to his tent around 6:00 P.M., Chomolunga had awakened with a hurricane-like blizzard in full force, mauling everyone in its path. Zero visibility in the whiteout conditions made each step a potential fall. The more than twenty people still high on the mountain stumbled down, teammates dragging near unconscious teammates in the dark, leaning hard into one hundred mile an hour winds. On the way back to the tents, a group of eleven climbers became hopelessly lost in the dark on the South Col. They wandered around for hours in the dark and freezing conditions, almost falling off the Kashung Face into Tibet.

Two days later, when the merciless storm finally subsided, both expedition leaders, Hall and Fischer, were confirmed dead as well as six other climbers. The elusive, dangerous beauty of Everest had proved herself once again.

Who would have thought?

Only days earlier in the wide glacial valley of the Western Cwm at the lower base camps, who would have thought that these expeditions were headed into a blinding, ferocious maelstrom? Though the guides and climbers knew that any attempt on Everest was dangerous, extremely dangerous, who would have thought the combination of unexpected events and crowded conditions would prove so lethal?

As I flipped to the last page of the book, a chill climbed up my spine. The story was so compelling; I was ready to turn back to page 1 to start all over again. Like millions of other Americans, I first followed the Everest tragedy in the news. When *Into Thin Air* hit the bookstores, I devoured it in front of a warm, crackling fire from the safety of my brown leather chair while drinking a fresh, hot cup of French roast. Krista, my wife, did make fun of me, though, for wearing my climbing harness as I read.

After finishing the book I quietly thanked God I didn't have to climb down the icy knife-edge of the Southeast Ridge in the dark, where a single misstep would have sent me cartwheeling seven thousand feet off the backside of Everest and into Tibet. I wiggled my fingers and appreciated the fact that our room temperature was not seventy degrees below zero, that I hadn't lost my glove, and that I was not Beck Weathers, whose hand turned into a frozen black stump that was later amputated

along with assorted other body parts. I was grateful I didn't
have to battle the subzero hurricane winds ready to flick me
down to base camp like an NHL hockey puck. Think about
it: All that wind and you *still* can't breathe.

Mountaintop experiences aren't always what they're cracked
up to be.

The 1996 Everest tragedy is a story about a group of people
with incredible aspirations and the best of intentions. The teams
aimed for the highest peak but they encountered the perfect
storm. Each expedition started out together but ended up di-
vided. They made plans and set goals for the top but broke com-
mitments and ignored responsibilities along the route. When the
sun was out and the way crystal clear, everyone on the team had
perfect direction, but when the storm hit, the climbers became
lost in search of shelter. In howling winds and blinding snow,
they leaned on friends for survival and security, only to be led
in the wrong direction. Many had dreamed about this adventure
for years, but nobody imagined it would come to this.

Why does Krakauer's story sound so eerily familiar? Maybe
because it is like so many marriages you and I know. Maybe
even your own marriage. Or mine. Think of all your married
friends. Go back a few years. Remember all the weddings you
attended? Then one day, you received a phone call. Or a friend
asked you to lunch. By the time the romaine salad had arrived,
you'd gotten the news.

It's all over. Finished. Kaput.

Who would have thought?

I don't believe for a second that anyone stands at the altar
before God, family, and friends, only to secretly conspire in
the deepest corner of their heart, *Let's see . . . how can I mess up
my marriage?*

Nobody thinks like that. Your friends don't. You don't. I don't.

What couple isn't like an Everest expedition party that wants
to climb to the highest peak and live on the thin air of love

15

alone? Who doesn't begin the adventurous journey of marriage eager to hit every relationship peak along the trail of spending a lifetime together in love? What couple doesn't want to reach the mountaintop of companionship? The summit of friendship? The pinnacle of belonging? The climax of intimacy? The highest peak of unconditional love?

Like many other tragedies we see on the news and read in the paper, the Everest tragedy triggered an avalanche of debate, books, articles, and lawsuits. And lots of Monday-morning quarterbacking. What if, before the storm hit, the Everest climbers had the advantage of another viewpoint? What if one of the climbers could have hopped into a helicopter (though impossible at such heights) and stood on the nearby peaks of Yhotse or Ama Dablam to see the changing weather patterns? What if the teams maintained the personal discipline to stick to the original agreed-upon plan? What if all expedition members shared the greater values of safety and relationship instead of the success and recognition that accompanies climbing the world's highest mountain?

Or better yet, what if in the middle of the raging storm, the biting winds, and the whiteout conditions, the weary mountaineers were given an extra bottle of oxygen? A free, unconditional offer of warmth and shelter? A more excellent way? Do you think they'd take it?

In a heartbeat.

What about you? What if you were offered a more excellent way? In the midst of your most perfect marriage storm, what if you were offered a free, unconditional path of safety and security instead of teetering over

> Who doesn't begin the adventurous journey of marriage eager to hit every relationship peak along the trail of spending a lifetime together in love?

the edge of the scary route you're on? What if someone offered to lighten your load? A personal porter. Your own Sherpa to schlepp your stuff down the mountain. To show you a better way. A more excellent way. Would you choose it if you knew you wouldn't have to go it alone?

> What if you were offered a more excellent way?

Maybe you're not in the middle of a marriage maelstrom; maybe you're having a relaxing picnic on a beautiful peak somewhere. But whatever the condition of your marriage, we all need a more excellent way. As much as we'd like to think we could, you and I can't live on the thin air of love alone. No matter how long you've been married—one week, one year, fifty years—no marriage lives on love alone. Of course, it sounds nice. Very romantic. Just like a mountaintop experience. A great vantage point where you can hold hands. Pop open a bottle of bubbly. But a mountaintop is no place to set up camp. We can visit the peaks, but we can't stay. Life doesn't work like that.

We can't camp on the peaks, because the weather conditions are always changing. Ask any Everest expedition. The truth of all marriages and all relationships is that they are filled with changing weather patterns. It is our choices, the choices of our spouses, and the ever-shifting circumstances encountered in day-to-day living that create and contribute to the ever-changing climatic conditions of our relationships. Marriage is a lot more than love alone, and it requires far more than you and I ever imagined when we first began the journey.

Contrary to popular thinking, love is not something you fall into or out of. True love is not an arbitrary impulse that hits us like a Tomahawk missile in the back of the head. Love is a choice . . . *our choice* . . . and love is a lot of hard work. Unlike the weather, which you and I can't control, love is a choice within our control. We can choose to love or we can choose not to. We can work at loving and becoming more loving in all of our relationships. Or choose not to. The weather reporter on Channel 7 can only predict. You get to decide. If you don't want to work at love and make the choices necessary to improve the conditions in your marriage, this book is probably not for you. There. I said it. That's my one condition: To develop a deeper love in your marriage, you have to be willing to work. (That includes your spouse. . . . I know what some of you are already thinking: *I'm willing to work, but Immortal Beloved over here isn't!*)

But let's be honest here. Who wants to work? Work's not any fun! After all, if we're really in love, shouldn't our love just work? We're soul mates, for crying out loud. We "complete" one another! If we have to work at love, maybe we're not in love after all.

Well, we all want to be loved, but love *is* a lot of work. That's where the rub comes in. Love is the reason we get hitched in the first place, isn't it? (Except for when large amounts of money are involved.) Isn't that the whole point? To live in love? To love another without condition? To look into the eyes of our beloved and whisper with everything in us, "I love you unconditionally"?

That's precisely the point. And that's precisely the problem. We are filled with love and our love is filled with conditions. Our love has more conditions than the Weather Channel's national broadcast. Our love rises in the morning bright and cheery like sunny Southern California. By noon, it's isolated clouds and a few scattered thundershowers over the Rockies. Then we drift into the overcast drab of Midwest melancholy at four. By the

> Love is a choice . . . our choice . . . and love is a lot of hard work.

six o'clock news, we slide right into sleet and snow in the East. Then it's off to bed with a huff and a grump.

Though unconditional love is our ideal, we're not very good at it, to be honest. We are quite unpredictable in how we understand love, practice love, give love, and receive love. When Immortal Beloved acts less than lovely — okay, like a big fat jerk or jerkess — we change like the wind. We blow up like a volcano. Too much conflict and we begin to harden like a hailstone. We become bitter like acid rain. Our hearts begin to look a lot like, well, Seattle.

And this is what gives unconditional love such a bad rap. It sounds so impossible. So unattainable. That's because unconditional love is too often misunderstood as a conditional love with no limits. A love that knows no boundary or restriction. A love that puts up with anything or everything. A love that never has to change. People talk about unconditional love as if it is the sugary red and blue syrup we pour on snow cones. *If I am just really sweet and pour my unconditional love all over my spouse, then all of our problems will melt away.* Actually, no. Now you have a spouse with a purple tongue.

I am not advocating the dysfunctional understanding of unconditional love that is possessive, needy, clingy, controlling, or all-giving. Unconditional love has limits, borders, and boundaries. In regard to certain behaviors and choices, true unconditional love sets limits, and so should we. Unconditional love does not allow an abuser to keep abusing, a control freak to keep controlling, and an enabler to keep enabling. True unconditional love can and must say, "Stop it or else." It can also say, "Wait. Not now. We'll see. Let's talk it over or let's sleep on it." Unconditional love is not a sentimental journey into wishful thinking; it comes from a power and source outside ourselves. Unconditional love is not living with Tunnel of Love tunnel vision; it enables us to keep our hearts wide open to new possibilities, options, choices, and discoveries.

Even in a perfect world, Eden, love had its limits. God told Adam and Eve that there was one thing they should know: *Go enjoy everything I have created, but there's one tree that's off limits. That is my one condition.*

Even God has his one condition; love does have its limits. But Adam and Eve wanted nothing to do with God's one condition. One fruit smoothie later, and we're left with the rotten apples of conditional love. Now, though the goal may be unconditional love, every marriage has its conditions. Like the weather, some are good and some are bad. Certain important conditions are necessary to make a marriage grow and thrive. Like the weather report, conditions tell us how we're doing and how we're getting along. But unlike the weather, the conditions we create in our marriages are often dependent on our choices. Good choices create good conditions and a positive environment of growth and change. Poor choices can create increasingly unfavorable conditions that cause good marriages to go bad.

Our power to choose is what makes us distinctly human. This power comes from God. In our marriages, God sets before us the option of living with our conditional love or by the power of his unconditional love. In calling the people of Israel to choose the amazing, unconditional love of God, Moses put forth this challenge to the Israelites:

> Unconditional love has limits, borders, and boundaries. In regards to certain behaviors and choices, true unconditional love sets limits, and so should we.

This day I call heaven and earth as witnesses against you that I have set before you life and death, blessings and curses. Now choose life, so that you and your children may live and that you may love the LORD your God, listen to his voice, and hold fast to him. For the LORD is your life.

Deuteronomy 30:19–20

God gave the people of Israel his law. It was a very long legal covenant detailing the very specific terms and conditions for the moral, religious, social, and political life of Israel. In the law, God outlined how the Israelites were to love and obey him by following his commandments. By loving and obeying God, the Israelites were promised abundant blessings. By breaking their covenant with God, the Israelites brought curses and captivity upon themselves. They had this thing for doing laps in the desert.

Since the Israelites were unable to keep God's law, God offered them a better way, a more excellent way. He promised the Israelites a Messiah, someone who would come not to do away with the law but to fulfill it with the law of love. The Messiah would come to bring all men and women—all marriages—back into relationship with God. Following God's Son, Jesus Christ—the Way, the Truth, and the Life—was to be the new standard for walking in the most excellent way of love.

When Jesus was asked what was the greatest commandment in the law, he replied, "'Love the Lord your God with all your heart and with all your soul and with all your mind.' This is the first and greatest commandment. And the second is like it: 'Love your neighbor as yourself.' All the Law and the Prophets hang on these two commandments" (Matt. 22:37–40).

Moses had the ten conditions, um, commandments. Jesus gave us a break and reduced it to two. I appreciate his willingness to work with me, but if I can't keep the Ten Commandments, what makes me think I can keep the two commandments? Those two commandments are a bit all-encompassing, aren't they? If I'm to love God and love my neighbor as myself, which I'm almost positive includes my wife, Krista, I'm going to need something more than my conditional love. I don't know about you, but I can't do it on my own power. Fortunately, there is a more excellent way: following the Way.

Before Jesus left this earth, he promised he would not leave you and me alone. He promised to leave us with a Counselor, Comforter, and Friend. He promised us his Holy Spirit, the most experienced "love guide" we could ever ask for. Better than the most experienced Everest expedition guide — and God isn't charging sixty-five thousand dollars a head for a million-dollar view of his world.

The Holy Spirit promises to guide you in the most excellent way of love. Through the highest highs and lowest lows. Through the laughter and through the looney bin. Through the messy, mucky, mundane world that every marriage goes through. By following the more excellent way of the Spirit, you will be able to overcome the most difficult marriage storms and experience new possibilities for the weather patterns of your most persistent problems. As you keep in step with the Spirit, you will discover that he has the power to change your heart and your marriage. Whether you are walking on the peak or through the valley right now, the Holy Spirit will give you the power to make choices that can actually change the condition of your heart and the conditions you create in your marriage.

And as you navigate your way through the pages of this book, you'll discover we are going to travel through the valleys before we get to the peaks, which I trust makes this a very unconventional marriage book. Part 1 is written for us to talk about the nature of unconditional love — its meaning in valleys where we live and work and what makes it so difficult to keep choosing love through the trials of everyday living. Part 2 gets more specific, providing anchors to be set for the climb ahead and offering you the more excellent pathway of 1 Corinthians 13. If our marriages are going to be filled with conditions, these are the conditions that we want to live by. The greatest words ever written on love are found in this famous chapter, and by choosing to live by these conditions, your heart will not only find safety but hopefully get in the best condition it's ever been in.

Will you take this most excellent way of love? Let's step out of the storm and follow God's lead. Let's get off this peak and journey to the valley below.

The valley is where the oxygen is thick and plentiful.

It's where you and I were made to live.

Whether you are walking on the peak or through the valley right now, the Holy Spirit will give you the power to make choices that can actually change the condition of your heart and the conditions you create in your marriage.

I Love You
Unconditionally...

CHAPTER ONE

A View
of the Valley

It is not a new scene which is needed, but a new viewpoint.

Norman Rockwell

At the end of last summer, Krista and I went with our kids to Big Bear Lake in the local Southern California Mountains. We looked forward to hiking Castle Rock, fishing off a pontoon boat, taking long naps, and exploring the beauty of God's creation. We were eager to get away for a few days before school started, before the busy fall routine of preparing lunches, doing homework, and attending after-school sports. Who doesn't love getting out of the valley and away from it all for a few short days?

Driving up the twisting mountain road, I was repeatedly reminded by my kids to "stay between the lines." On a camping trip to Big Bear the previous summer, I was pulled over by a cordial police officer for swerving and crossing the double yellow lines. As I sat in the front seat and prayed like a mouse in a snake pit, Ellie yelled from the backseat, "Hey, Dad, he's writing on a thick pad of paper."

"That's not good," I said. The cordial police officer refused to let me make this a teaching opportunity for my kids about unconditional love and undeserved grace. He insisted I give him my autograph. Viper. I can't blame him, though. He was just doing his job, ticketing a dad taking his kids camping instead of doing real police work like catching drug lords and serial killers.

I admit I crossed the double yellow lines, with malice and a flagrant disregard for the law. Not that I'm bitter or anything. I just don't know which is worse: traffic school or a bunch of junior drivers' ed instructors in the backseat warning me about California's Three Strikes law and the high cost of auto insurance premiums.

This time we made it up the mountain road without any repeat offenses. After a couple days, we went into town for lunch at a local eatery known for its strong coffee and delicious baked goods. While Krista ordered lunch, I walked over to a bulletin board to check out the local advertisements and the dozens of colored papers pinned to the rectangle of corkboard. In the middle of the board, held fast by a red pushpin, someone had stuck a quote from Norman Rockwell. "Common places never become tiresome. It is we who become tired when we cease to be curious and appreciative. We find that it is not a new scene which is needed, but a new viewpoint."

Thank you, Norman, I said to myself and scrounged around for something to write with. A purple crayon and a scrap of paper. I slipped Rockwell's point of view into the pocket of my blue jeans.

Our three days in Big Bear flashed by, and before we knew it, we were twisting back and forth down the mountain road, heading back to the valley. Between the lines, of course. We had a wonderful little vacation. A mini-mountaintop experience.

In the lifelong journey of marriage, every couple needs time on the mountain peaks, because mountaintop experiences help us to see where we've been and where we're going. Mountain-top experiences help us to reconnect and revisit why we married each other in the first place. These special times are essential for the commitment, enthusiasm, and longevity of every marriage. A romantic dinner. Intimate conversation. A fun vacation. Dreaming together about the future. Celebrating each other's victories. Cherishing each other's unique qualities.

No marriage can survive without the rest, relaxation, and restoration found in mountaintop experiences, but what I'm learning and relearning throughout my journey with my wife is that a marriage cannot survive on the thin air of peak experiences. Vacations are for getting away from the valley. An escape from the humdrum. A respite from the day-in, day-out routine of life. The get-me-outta-here pressures that suck the life out of us. No more deadlines. No more stress. No more responsibilities. No more more.

As much as we want and need mountaintop experiences, the thick, plentiful air is found in the valley. The valley is the place of growth because we grow where the soil is most fertile. In the valleys. In the muck. The messes. The mundaneness of everyday living. Vacation offers us needed rest and a change of scenery, but a change of scenery won't change our lives. Or our marriages. Real meaning and connection and purpose are sustained in the valley, not on vacation.

> As much as we want and need mountaintop experiences, the thick, plentiful air is found in the valley.

Here, Rockwell is instructive: What we need is a new viewpoint. A new viewpoint for how we look at love and marriage in the valley of everyday life. The new viewpoint that I find helpful, one I try to remind myself of often, is this: A loving marriage is created and shaped, molded and nurtured, tested and sustained in the valleys of life. Not on the mountaintops. The majesty and awesomeness of the mountaintops can help us see how small our problems really are in the grand scope of life, but the valleys don't let us off the hook that easily. In the valleys, we are confronted with our choices, our consequences, and ultimately, the true condition of our hearts. In the valleys, we're confronted with the conditional nature of our love.

The real work of love, the hard work, takes place in the valleys. The grit and growth of marriage happen in the shallow lowlands of our fears and conditional love, where the land must be worked, the soil tilled, our gardens weeded; where we face choices, temptations, and challenges.

The valley is where life is at. It's where you and I wake up and go to bed every day of our lives without room service or a personal concierge. No seaweed mud spa treatments or unlimited golf packages. It's where life is pretty common. Yes, even boring. It's in your kitchen and mine. It's in the sacred chore of making peanut butter and jelly sandwiches and screaming at the kids to get down for breakfast. Life is in trying to figure out the opposite species you married and wiping up the spilled milk and Cheerios all over the floor. Those sacred Cheerios—little circly signs of life. Life is in the nine-to-five routine of waking early and arguing over Leno and Letterman late at night. It's in dropping off and picking up at

> A loving marriage is created and shaped, molded and nurtured, tested and sustained in the valleys of life. Not on the mountaintops.

airports and schools. In minivan traffic madness and SUV smog. Life is in sitting at church and standing in line at Starbucks. At work and family gatherings. It's in our worries and working out at the club. In Legos and lunch boxes, in Barbies and broken hearts. In tenderness and tears. Fighting and forgiving. Loving and learning.

> God is the giver of life, and he is the creator of the peaks and the valleys. . . . He is "God with us" in the daily grind as we pour our first cup to start a new day.

God is the giver of life, and he is the creator of the peaks and the valleys. He is the One who gives breath, sustains breath, and takes our breath away. His best work is done in the valleys where we eat, work, and play. Where the oxygen is thick and plentiful. He is "God with us" in the daily grind as we pour our first cup to start a new day.

Every couple, at some point in time, becomes tired and restless in their marriage. Why? Rockwell hints that we've ceased to be curious and appreciative. I think he's right. The moment we cease to be curious and appreciative about life and one another, we're headed for that ditch on the side of the road known as a rut. We take life and one another for granted, missing out on the mystery wrapped in every unfolding day.

This is when we get into trouble: when we stop looking for new viewpoints. Sometimes we get so stuck in the rhythm of our routines that we forget to stop and check if we're on the right road, headed together in the same direction. And before we know it, we're wandering down paths that distract and divide our hearts from one another and the greater journey before us.

If you feel overwhelmed by living in the valley, you're not alone. It's my hope that this book encourages you along the way. Getting to the peaks, the high points of marriage where we power into a good groove, takes work. And it begins with key choices made in the valley. The mountains have their inherent dangers and so do the valleys. It's easy to be choked by the atmospheric pressure of life bearing down on us. At different points of the journey, it's easy to get tired and weary by the weight of this world. No one is immune to fatigue and weakness. So it's not uncommon to lose sense of why we started this marriage journey in the first place.

By avoiding the difficult reality in which we live, we can begin to believe that life is found in some other place. Anywhere but here. Another marriage, perhaps, but not this one. Real life is out there somewhere, far up on a distant peak or on an exotic tropical island where all we need to worry about is stirring a little blue umbrella in an overpriced fruity drink. Maybe on a boat in the Bahamas or some idealized world like a Danielle Steele or Tom Clancy novel in which boy meets girl, the sex is great, and love takes no work. But our illusions are what's really novel. If our illusions were best-sellers, we'd all be millionaires.

I'm convinced *Into Thin Air* needs to be required reading for every married couple in America, because it's a sobering tale that strips away our illusions about mountaintop experiences. *Into Thin Air* was a terrifying mountaintop experience. A reality none of us would ever want to face. Maybe we should call this book you're reading now *Into Thick Muck,* because that's where you and I live.

> If our illusions were best-sellers, we'd all be millionaires.

What you and I need are new choices based on a new perspective. New choices to change the conditions we live by. Remember Norman Rockwell's famous painting of the nervous boy looking over his shoulder, not wanting to drop his shorts, while a doctor in a white coat prepares a long, silver syringe for his bum? A new viewpoint can prick our attention and point us in the right direction for navigating the valleys where we live.

I'm in regular need of a new perspective for my marriage. Another angle. Outside input. I need more than the mechanics of marriage practicality. I need God to get in the middle of my life and my marriage with an authentic, transformational spirituality. Do you think our marriages might be a little more intimate, a little more loving, if we spent a little more time working on our vows instead of planning the next vacation? That's why we need someone to help us with living in the valley.

Let's face it: Marriage is dangerous work. I don't know about you, but when I'm about to do something dangerous, I want to be with someone who knows exactly what they're doing. I want to be with a pro. Someone with knowledge. Skill. Experience.

What I want is an expert for activities that have a high potential for death or dismemberment. Like the time I went white-water rafting. The moment I was told my white-water rafting guide was nineteen years old, I should have asked for a travel voucher. I had been invited to go white-water rafting with a youth group of middle school tweeners by a friend who, as I reflect on it now, cared little for my life.

We were at the Trinity River in Northern California. It was an El Niño year—the rainiest season on this planet, I think, since Noah bolted the door to the ark. Churning and frothing like a beast, the Trinity was twenty feet higher than usual, pulsating with liquid energy. The river reminded me of one of those beer commercials in which three or so boats charge down the rapids filled with laughing and smiling people because they are getting paid so much money to risk their life for a beer commercial.

We weren't laughing. No smiles. No beer. No getting paid the big bucks. With paddles in hand, we were charging for the most dangerous series of rapids. Each rapid had a pleasant, inviting name like Hellhole, Destroyer, or the Four Horsemen of the Apocalypse. And in the boat were me, four tweeners wetting their pants, and our nineteen-year-old river guide, whom we will christen "Irresponsible."

Fifty yards before we entered the rapids of no return, Irresponsible stood up and announced that he was heading to the front of our inflatable boat to sit on the bow and ride the rapid holding the "D-Ring," also known as the "Dimwit Ring." Irresponsible told me I was now assuming the *Love Boat* role of Captain Merrill Stubing and directed me to make sure we entered the rapid pointed downstream. Irresponsible was already at the bow with his legs thrown over the side, holding the Dimwit Ring between his legs like a bronco bull rider ready to burst into a corral.

I was feeling no love for Irresponsible, but I had no time to argue. Irresponsible was whooping and hollering, having a good ol' time. I was trying to steer, angling the boat in the right direction and yelling "Paddle!" to the tweeners, two of whom were crying for their mommy. My paddle was six feet long, and I was almost positive that with a good reach, I could whack Irresponsible on the head and lose the deadweight. Better his body than mine. It wouldn't show up for miles downstream.

Screaming for our lives, we plunged into a five-foot cascade of latte foam on the rocks. Instead of bouncing up when hitting the base of the drop, the weight of Irresponsible torpedoed the nose of the boat deep into the river. The boat jackknifed like a big rig on I-5. Captain Stubing and all the tweeners launched out of the Love Boat into the raging river filled with rocks, whirlpools, and irresponsible boat guides. Submerged, we ingested half of the Trinity, not quite ready to meet God in Three Persons. Eventually surfacing, we went with the flow downstream, our heads bobbing like apples in life jackets that I feared would soon be pulled off our dead bodies and placed on the next unsuspecting group of adventure seekers led by a river guide named Irresponsible.

The next time I go river rafting, I am going with someone I can trust. If I want to take a bath, I'll stay at home. If I want to hold my breath underwater, I'll do it in a Jacuzzi instead of a river with bubbles the size of basketballs. I will not leave my life in the hands of a nineteen-year-old with water on the brain. I want someone experienced who can lead with authority. Someone who has my personal interests and safety in mind. This is the exact kind of person I want to talk to about my love life.

Whether I'm on a mountain peak in my marriage, down in the valley, or at the bottom of a river struggling to come up for air, I want to talk with someone who knows what it's like to keep in step with the Spirit. Someone who has actually experienced the transformational power of God. Someone who knows how to lead, guide, instruct, and assist. Someone with a good viewpoint, the best viewpoint, who can help me make sense of the valley where I live. Someone who can pique my curiosity and offer me new choices to help change the conditional nature of my love. Someone like the apostle Paul.

If there's anyone who knows how to talk to us about what love is and what it is not, it's Paul. Perhaps you know his story?

He used to be called Saul.

CHAPTER TWO

Transformed by Love

If God can transform the life of a legalistic, self-righteous, murder-breathing inquisitor like Saul, what possibilities could there be for your life and marriage?

Before God flicked him off his high horse and transformed his life forever, Paul's actual name was Saul. He was a paid religious criminal of sorts, but his name wasn't changed because he was about to enter the Federal Witness Protection program. God had a different kind of witness program in mind.

As a brilliant and powerful Pharisee, Saul had it out for anyone who claimed to follow the Nazarene, the supposed resurrected leader of the Way. These people, these "Christ ones," irritated Saul like desert sand in his shorts. So he set out to make a change. He had one condition in mind.

Saul's terms were simple: If you admitted to being a follower of the Way, Saul said "No way" and set out to break you. He gave you two choices: denounce or die. There were no other conditions. Denounce the Way of love or eat rocks for lunch. Saul was present and accounted for at the rockfest stoning of Stephen—he worked the coat check for the murderers (Acts 7:58).

Immediately following the death of Stephen, conditions only got worse. A persecution of the church broke out in Jerusalem, and Saul was the leading henchman. "Saul began to destroy the church. Going from house to house, he dragged off men and women and put them in prison" (Acts 8:3). He was a man on a mission of destruction, using every trick in his bag. Lies. Murder and false testimony. Trumped-up charges. Kangaroo courts.

One day, Saul woke up with the familiar smell of murder on his breath. Christians for breakfast, maybe? He went to the high priest, requesting permission to cast his dragnet farther to catch the Christ ones in the town of Damascus and snatch them back to prison in Jerusalem. The high priest told him to go for it, and Saul set off into the desert on a horse with no name. The rest is history.

After coming face to face with Jesus, the very One whom he'd been persecuting, Saul was never the same. Joe Friday had names changed to protect the innocent, but Saul didn't have an innocent bone in his body. God changed his name from Saul to Paul to show everyone that the old Saul was dead. Gone. Finished. Jesus gave him a new condition to live by: the condition of God's unconditional love. The new Paul was transformed by the love and grace of God. With a change of heart came the power to make new choices. New choices that could lead to new conditions for his life. God's love transformed Saul—a powerful, self-righteous, murderbreathing mauler of lives and families—to Paul—a new man who would become God's chosen instrument for showing the world the Way.

You could say God placed Paul in a new type of witness protection program. The game plan was daunting, yet simple. God told Paul, "Be my witness. Show others the power that comes with a transformed life. Go and tell them of the unconditional, transforming love of my Son, Jesus Christ." This became Paul's life work. Though he always considered himself "the chiefest of sinners," he now knew who he was as a child of God. He knew in the deepest part of his heart that he was wholly loved and wholly forgiven. Paul didn't stay put on the metaphorical mountaintop experience of a powerful, life-changing encounter with the living God. He got to work and headed into the valley to be who God had called him to be and to do what God had called him to do.

Paul's story convinces me that he's the real deal. When it comes to learning more about conditional love and the unconditional, transforming love of God, I want to speak to a guy who knows what he's talking about. Some people put their money where their mouth is, but Paul went even further than that. So transforming was the love of God in his life, he endured constant hardship, suffering, and persecution. With the unconditional love of God in his heart, he made the daily choice to follow the Holy Spirit's lead in changing the broken condition of this world.

If anybody has earned the right to talk to us about love, it's Paul. Since he now counted himself a follower of Christ, he became the New Testament Fight Club poster child. As a murder-breathing religious leader in Jerusalem, he knew how to dish it out. Now he was on the receiving end. Run out of town. Numerous jail stints. Stoned. Bad boat luck—shipwrecked three times. Beaten like a dirty carpet with rods three times. Five times he received forty lashes minus one. After five rounds of thirty-nine lashings, who's counting?

I'll let Paul finish the story:

> I have been constantly on the move. I have been in danger
> from rivers, in danger from bandits, in danger from my own
> countrymen, in danger from Gentiles; in danger in the city,
> in danger in the country, in danger at sea; and in danger from
> false brothers. I have labored and toiled and have often gone
> without sleep; I have known hunger and thirst and have often
> gone without food; I have been cold and naked. Besides ev-
> erything else, I face daily the pressure of my concern for all
> the churches.
>
> *2 Corinthians 11:26–28*

All this for the love of God? Okay, Paul, you've earned your
stripes. Literally. You have our attention.

If God can transform the life of a legalistic, self-righteous,
murder-breathing inquisitor like Saul, what possibilities could
there be for your life and marriage? If you and I had been
able to see Saul in action ripping people from their homes,
dividing husbands and wives, separating parents from their
children, throwing them in jail, and applauding at executions,
would we have given him a shot at a transformed life? No
way, Jose.

Don't we sometimes say the same thing about ourselves?
Don't we sometimes look at the mess all around us and say the
same thing about our marriages? Can God get in the middle
of this muck? Can he make any difference at all? It's difficult
not to become cynical when the valley is filled with so much
smog. *Can God really get in the middle of my life here in the valley?
Does he even want to?*

The good news of the gospel is that God knows your heart,
and he does his best work with broken lives. He knows you
and I have a heart condition. In fact, the only kind of patients
Jesus sees are those with heart conditions. Haven't you seen
his business card?

39

Jesus Christ, cardiologist

New patients welcome

Offices worldwide

Heart transplants and reconstructive surgery

Though Jesus spent a few years in construction, eventually he was off to medical school and went into his Father's business. He said it himself, "Who needs a doctor: the healthy or the sick? I'm here inviting the sin-sick, not the spiritually-fit" (Mark 2:17 MESSAGE).

> Just as God transformed Paul's life, he wants to do the same with yours. And the way he begins transforming your life is by wooing you with his unconditional love.

"But you don't know my husband . . . you don't know my wife. You don't know what we've been through and what our marriage is like." No, I don't know what your marriage is like. I won't pretend to be an expert on your pain. But I do know that God is in the business of transforming lives. Whether your marriage is great or going down the tubes, God isn't finished with you yet. Just as God transformed Paul's life, he wants to do the same with yours. And the way he begins transforming your life is by wooing you with his unconditional love. You may just see the mess and feel all the muck you're wading through, but God is quite artistic. He can make much out of mud pies.

Still not convinced? That's okay. Let's let God speak for himself. When we turn to him, God promises to transform our hearts.

> I will give you a new heart and put a new spirit in you; I will
> remove from you your heart of stone and give you a heart of
> flesh. And I will put my Spirit in you and move you to follow
> my decrees and be careful to keep my laws. . . . You will be my
> people, and I will be your God.
>
> *Ezekiel 36:26–28*

The essence of the Christian life is spiritual transformation. It begins with sinners, not saints. And a transformed heart leads to a changed life. Oh, we can grudgingly muster up our own strength to be more patient, loving, and kind, even when we're feeling as nasty as a rattlesnake, but we can't mistake tolerance for authentic transformational love.

With a new heart and God's Spirit in us, we now have God's power to love our spouses in a transformational way. God promises us his Holy Spirit to give us the power to make choices we'd be powerless to make on our own. We were created to love God, to be in relationship with him and with one another. The only way we can be in relationship with him is to be transformed by the richness of his love. And this is what he delights to give us. Isaiah 62:5 says, "As a bridegroom rejoices over his bride, so will your God rejoice over you."

God rejoices in giving you his love. Pretty amazing, isn't it?

All the resources of God's power and his unconditional love provide us a more excellent way for making new choices in our marriages. The new perspective we need as God works in us to create the new conditions of unconditional love. The split-second point of view that

> All the resources of God's power and his unconditional love provide us a more excellent way for making new choices in our marriages.

keeps us from brandishing our tongues like a flamethrower. The strength to stay and work through a conflict when we feel like bolting. The graciousness to look at a problem from our husband's or wife's perspective and find the grace to appreciate it.

Just as Paul's back flip off his horse was the start of a whole new life, your spiritual transformation marks the beginning of a whole new journey. It doesn't matter if you've been a follower of the Way for years or if you're like a wobbly toddler on your toes: None of us is finished. None of our marriages is finished. The journey from the conditional love we know so well to the transforming, unconditional love of God is the journey of a lifetime. When God knocked Paul off his horse, Paul didn't just sit in a rut on the side of the road. He began to walk a life of faith, not really knowing where it would lead. In his travels spreading the good news of Jesus Christ throughout the Mediterranean, Paul had no idea what he was going to encounter along the way. Especially in the city of Corinth.

If there was one church that made Paul blush, it was the church in Corinth. Located in southern Greece, Corinth was a bustling Roman capital city and commercial center. It boasted a global marketplace—the Vanity Fair of the ancient world or, as some would call it, the Lounge of Greece. Corinth had some pretty peculiar notions about love, kind of like the world we live in today. The reigning Corinthian mantra was simple. It was based on the Corinthian Chamber of Commerce motto: When in Corinth, do as the drunken, debased, sex-crazed Corinthians do—just do it! (The Corinthian Chamber of Commerce is still in litigation with Nike regarding international trademark law over this matter.)

What made Corinth such a popular place was this little Love Shack up on the hill called the Temple of Aphrodite, dedicated to the goddess of love . . . er, lust. The temple was a major player in Corinth's international sex marketplace, which was long before the city ever had a web site.

This was what Paul was up against when he wrote a letter to the church in Corinth. Filled with new followers of the Way, the church had problems that mirrored the sins and sensuality of the city. You can dismiss any idealistic dreams about wanting to go back to the old times and worship in a New Testament church; the church at Corinth was not a sparkling bride in white standing before God at the altar. More often than not, the Corinthian church, like the church today, veered across the double lines. It was surrounded by a lot of confusing ideas about love, and it was filled with division and infighting. Spiritual immaturity and rampant immorality. Adultery. Idolatry. Divorce. Drunkenness. Thieves. Slanderers. When attendance was down on Sunday mornings, maybe it was because a few too many had wandered off the path up to Aphrodite's Love Shack.

But Paul, like the God he worshipped, loved the Corinthian church. Yes, God loves his church. Your church and mine. Even those crazy Corinthians. And he loves marriages. Marriages marred with mistakes. Marriages just trying to make it. God established his church as a place for sinners in need of transformation. And in loving his church, God spoke through Paul to show us a better way. A more excellent way.

Paul wrote the most famous words ever written on the subject of love. He wrote straight to the heart of the Corinthian people, a group of married couples and individuals who were pretty confused about the difference between conditional love and unconditional love. Paul penned his words smack dab in the valley of everyday life. "They want to

> God established his church as a place for sinners in need of transforming. And in loving his church, God spoke through Paul to show us a better way. A more excellent way.

43

know what real love is?" Paul said to himself. "Okay, I'll spell it out for them."

The Corinthians needed help just like we need help. The hope and encouragement God offered to the Corinthians through Paul is the same inspiration God offers to you and me today. Paul's life is living proof of the choices and powerful changes that can occur when God gets in the middle of a willing heart. But to understand the choices we can make that will change the conditions in our marriages, we first have to understand the true condition of our hearts. Like any good physician, Jesus wants us to know this so we'll be convinced that he really has the cure.

Paul's letter of love to the Corinthians and his words found in 1 Corinthians 13 provide us the context for understanding our condition and the cure. Let's follow Paul's lead down into the valley.

I'll try to stay between the lines, but watch out for the yak bells.

Serious road hazards.

CHAPTER THREE

Yak Bell Love

The weather conditions of my heart are so unpredictable, changing my BVDs has far more predictability.

Hidden deep in Heidi's backpack was a gift. But I wasn't interested in the gift; I wanted to see her photos of Nepal. I wanted to see the picture of Mount Everest against a cobalt blue sky. But my kids? They wanted the goods — the hidden gift. Heidi reached into her backpack and handed a small package to my daughter Ellie.

"Here you go," Heidi said with a smile. "I brought you back a little something from Nepal."

Ellie ripped open the package, much to Heidi's delight. It was good to see Heidi smile. A few years earlier she'd weathered the most difficult storm of her life. A Mt. Everest–sized tragedy. So much unnecessary pain. Rejection. Separation. A journey she'd never planned on. It was no small miracle to see Heidi happy, even hopeful, about her future.

I'll never forget the deflated, empty expression on Heidi's face during those dark years of her divorce. It was as if some-

one had walked up with a big pin and popped her. Left with
shattered dreams and a fractured future, Heidi couldn't sleep.
She couldn't eat. She lost weight. Not exactly the diet plan
most women want to go on.

Ellie opened the small package and pulled out a round golden
object. "What is it, Heidi?"

Heidi smiled and took it from Ellie's hand. "It's a yak bell
. . . see!" She waved the yak bell above her head, filling the
room with a loud, clunky sound.

A yak bell, I thought. How nice.

Ellie laughed and grabbed the black strap attached to the
bell, yanking it from Heidi, and thus proceeded to yak it around
the room at maximum volume. Joseph and Aidan jumped in
and took turns yakking the bell.

"Hey, hey!" I cried above the din. "Why don't you guys hike
to Nepal and play with that thing?"

Don't you love it when people buy your kids loud toys?

As all storms do, Heidi's eventually subsided. And out of her
pain came new perspectives. Lessons learned. Even a handsome man named Chris. The rock on Heidi's finger wasn't of
the Mt. Everest variety. Heidi was looking forward to starting
a new life with Chris. A new marriage. A new route. A more
excellent way.

The apostle Paul, our appointed love guide, promised to
show us a more excellent way for developing deeply intimate
and loving relationships. In writing 1 Corinthians 13, also
known as "the love chapter," Paul penned the most famous
words ever written on the subject of love. By comparison,
Cupid's love arrow misses by a mile. And I have yet to see
a Top Forty love song stay at the top of the charts for two
thousand years.

What is this most excellent way, you say? If 1 Corinthians
13 wasn't read at your wedding, you've heard it at every other
wedding you've ever been to. It offers an irresistible way of

love. Written almost two thousand years ago, it is as fresh and challenging and inspiring as ever. It reads rather *lovely.*

> If I speak in the tongues of men and of angels, but have not love, I am only a resounding gong or a clanging cymbal. [Or yak bell.] If I have the gift of prophecy and can fathom all mysteries and all knowledge, and if I have a faith that can move mountains, but have not love, I am nothing. If I give all I possess to the poor and surrender my body to the flames, but have not love, I gain nothing.
>
> Love is patient, love is kind. It does not envy, it does not boast, it is not proud. It is not rude, it is not self-seeking, it is not easily angered, it keeps no record of wrongs. Love does not delight in evil but rejoices with the truth. It always protects, always trusts, always hopes, always perseveres.
>
> Love never fails. But where there are prophecies, they will cease; where there are tongues, they will be stilled; where there is knowledge, it will pass away. For we know in part and we prophesy in part, but when perfection comes, the imperfect disappears. When I was a child, I talked like a child, I thought like a child, I reasoned like a child. When I became a man, I put childish ways behind me. Now we see but a poor reflection as in a mirror; then we shall see face to face. Now I know in part; then I shall know fully, even as I am fully known.
>
> And now these three remain: faith, hope and love. But the greatest of these is love.

Paul penned the most famous words ever written on the subject of love. By comparison, Cupid's love arrow misses by a mile. And I have yet to see a Top Forty love song stay at the top of the charts for two thousand years.

Paul has provided us a more excellent way for navigating the journey of married life. First Corinthians 13 gives you and me clear direction for our choices and the conditions we choose to create in our marriages. Choices only you can choose to make. Choices only your spouse can choose to make. Conditions to create in our marriages and conditions to cut out of our marriages.

In 1 Corinthians 13, Paul points us to God, who shows us the wide expanse of his love—a completely different point of view from the one we are so familiar with. It's the difference between looking at the Grand Canyon and looking into a Coke can.

God is the author of love, and the qualities of love listed here are not only his perspective on the true nature of his love but also a mysterious glimpse into his very nature. John, the beloved follower of Jesus, wrote this about God: "God is love. Whoever lives in love lives in God, and God in him" (1 John 4:16). God offers us an incredible view of who he is and the love available to us. "Come on up," he says. "This is the path to walk, the most excellent way to live and love you've ever imagined."

God is inviting you to look at life, to look at your marriage from his vantage point. He's saying it's possible to love like he loves. You see, God's greatest desire is to write his love story into your life with the qualities of love found in 1 Corinthians 13.

> God is inviting you to look at life, to look at your marriage from his vantage point.

And this is where I begin to feel a bit overwhelmed. There's a lot of syrupy talk about unconditional love, but I, for one, know my love is filled with conditions. The weather conditions of my heart are so unpredictable, changing my BVDs has far more predictability. One moment I'm like a refreshing summer breeze; the next I'm as touchy as tiptoeing across baking hot sand at the beach. When I read 1 Corinthians 13, I know I don't measure up.

I'm sincerely patient and sincerely unkind. Grateful and envious. Humble as Mother Teresa and proud as Muhammad Ali. Really nice and stinkin' rude. I try to keep my record of wrongs shorter than my wife's Costco grocery list. I wish I could say my love never fails, but I know myself a little too well. I'd love to be able to say that I love Krista unconditionally, but the best I can say is that I love her unconditionally . . . on one condition.

I've got my condition, and you've got yours.

Our conditions are a lot like yak bells. Like gongs or cymbals, they don't make very good music. As much as I love my wife and want our marriage to be a symphony of love, to be quite honest, there are a lot of days when all I play is "Ode to a Yak Bell." When Paul wrote about resounding gongs and clanging cymbals, he didn't specifically mention yak bells, but he did say that we should put our love where our lips are and show love instead of yakking about it.

If you want to "be in love," you must love by choosing love. Practicing love. Demonstrating love. Making love is the easy part. After many years of marriage, I've discovered that my conditions create many of our postnuptial disagreements. Maybe you can relate to a few? Spoken or silent, a lot of the unfavorable conditions we set in our marriages sound like this:

"I will love you if you . . . *clank*."

"If you really loved me, you would . . . *clunk*."

"Is that how you show me you love me . . . *clanketty-clunk*."

"Why can't you be more like . . . *clunk-clunk*."

"If I did that to you, you would . . . *clank-clunk*."

We all have conditions, and they all go clunk.

I wish I could look into the deep pools of my wife's blue eyes and say that I love her unconditionally. That's the goal, but in my own power, I can't. I love Krista as best I know how, but the reality is that my love is too filled with conditions. My love has more terms and conditions than your average car rental agreement.

I am not Don Rico Suave.

Whenever I hear someone say, "I love my spouse unconditionally," I raise an eyebrow. I think of two words: *newlywed* or *liar*. No one loves unconditionally because no one is perfect. That's why every marriage has and needs conditions . . . the right conditions for love to grow and thrive. Our vows are conditions. The promises we make to one another are conditions. We need conditions for marriage precisely because we don't know how to love unconditionally. The vows and covenants we commit our lives to are the conditions that serve as a perimeter wall around our hearts to protect our marriage from the destructive choices and conditions that can destroy our lives.

I'm far more familiar with clanging yak bells, gonging gongs, and clashing cymbals, because that's what I grew up with. My mom occasionally took me and my sisters and brother to the Huntington Library. (I say "occasionally" because try to imagine yourself chasing seven screaming children through a hoity-toity museum and manicured gardens the size of the Rose Bowl.) My favorite part of the Huntington Library was the Japanese garden. Yes, I am admitting I was a huge Kung Fu fan. Anyway, in the center of the quiet, serene Japanese garden was an enormous bronze gong the size of a large trash dumpster. Next to the gong, hanging on brown leather straps, was a long, four-by-four log used to gong the gong.

> My love has more terms and conditions than your average car rental agreement. I am not Don Rico Suave.

The moment us O'Connor kids stepped inside the Japanese garden, there was a mad dash to see who would get to the gong first. Scattered throughout the garden were park visitors sitting on stone benches, sipping tea, getting into some sort of Zen vibe, enjoying a quiet lunch hour, and taking in the peaceful beauty of the surroundings.

> Whenever I hear someone say, "I love my spouse unconditionally," I raise an eyebrow. I think of two words: *newlywed* or *liar.*

That was my cue to pull back that big old log and let 'er rip. *Ka-gooong!*

Not once, of course.

Ka-gooong! Ka-gooong! Ka-gooong!

By the time my mom got to us, the garden was emptied, and I'm almost positive the Huntington Library lost at least a couple major donors.

Not only did Japanese gongs have a significant influence on my career as a yak bell musical artist, but my dad also had an influence. He played the cymbals in the San Marino Fourth of July marching band, and as a second grader, I thought to myself, *How cool is that!* I mean, how many dads get chosen to play the cymbals in the Fourth of July parade marching band? My kids loved Heidi's yak bell, and I loved smashing my dad's cymbals. The louder the better. I remember bragging to my buddies, "My dad's playing the cymbals in the Fourth of July marching band!" It didn't get any better than that. Except for the fireworks, of course.

And that's what we want from our spouses. We want the fireworks. Batta-bing! Batta-bang! We want the sparks. A colorful, vibrant marriage. Lots of sizzle. But the conditions we create and the unrealistic expectations we place on one another

51

sometimes cause our love to fizzle. The Fourth of July picnic we plan for our lives gets bogged down under the weight of poor choices. Our love doesn't naturally sustain itself. It can't sustain itself, because what our hearts know best and have experienced many times over is conditional love. You know it well. So do I.

Conditional love is the way of this world, and no one is immune to its influence. From the time you were a child, you learned love for performance. Love for keeping the rules. Love for keeping silent. Love for fulfilling the expectations of Mom or Dad. Love for straight As. Love for scoring touchdowns. Love for money. Love for making someone else happy. Love for keeping family secrets. Love for sex. Love for going along with the crowd. Love for trying to be someone else.

Linger on all those conditions of love. Fill in the blank. Go ahead.

I have been loved for_____.

Love is always for something, but it's never free. It is love at a cost. What our hearts know best and what the accumulation of our experiences since childhood have confirmed is that what we've been conditioned to respond to is conditional love. Love with limitations. Love as a payment plan for the heart. Love at 21 percent interest. Love mixed with control and expectations, which in many cases were misguided attempts at loving by well-meaning family and friends who were loved by the same conditions. Even in the best of homes, the best love was conditional love.

Theologically speaking, we were born into sin and stand separate from God. Our broken nature is evident in our inability to love as God loves. From our broken nature come the thoughts, attitudes, and actions that flow from a broken heart. Can parents love their children deeply and provide the close bonding and attachment every child needs? Without a doubt. But we're still broken.

So we enter marriage knowing all the terms and conditions of conditional love as we've experienced it, but then we are told to love without condition. Sounds like we've got a dilemma. If all we've experienced is conditional love, how can we possibly give the unconditional love our husband or wife desires? If all we know is conditional love, how can we learn to receive unconditional love without conditions? We hear a love song on the radio. Read a romance novel. Watch a blockbuster love story DVD. We hear lots of talk about falling in love, being in love, and staying in love. Great! Sign me up. That's what I want. That's what you want. But how?

In describing the love our hearts desire in 1 Corinthians 13, Paul points to both the need of our hearts and the condition of our hearts. Our deepest need is for unconditional love. The truest thing about us is our deep, insatiable ache to be loved and to belong. To be wholly accepted for who we are. To be cherished. To be told we are worthy of love without condition simply because we matter.

You want to be loved like this, don't you?

But the condition of our hearts, what we really know as Paul describes it, is obvious. Our hearts are impatient, unkind, envious, boastful, prideful, easily angered, and self-seeking, ad infinitum. Our hearts are sinful and separated from God, and we will never be able to get what we need until we are convinced of our true need. Our love fails because we have heart

If all we've experienced is conditional love, how can we possibly give the unconditional love our husband or wife desires? If all we know is conditional love, how can we learn to receive unconditional love without conditions?

failure. Though we are made in the image of God, the Bible says that apart from Jesus Christ, we don't have a spiritual pulse. Hook up any one of our hearts to an EKG machine and you'll see that we are spiritually and relationally flatlined. And it is impossible for us to resuscitate our own hearts. Trying to love unconditionally is as crazy as expecting someone in cardiac arrest to perform CPR on themselves. It just can't be done.

The truest thing about us is our need for unconditional love, yet we can't create this love on our own. And this is where Paul points the way. First Corinthians 13 is the beautiful picture of God's unconditional love available to you and me. Paul points to the pinnacle of love, the highest ideal of what love is all about, and tells us we cannot give what we have not first received. The message of God's love letter to you is simple:

God loves you unconditionally . . . on one condition.

Yes, even God has his one condition, but being God does have its privileges.

Here's his condition: Accept the free gift of his love.

From his love flows all the power to make new choices and create the new conditions you desire in your life and marriage. From his love comes the power to love unconditionally as you learn to drop your conditions in favor of the new conditions he wants to create in your heart and life. And saying yes to God is the only way to travel the journey of unconditional love. If you want a loving marriage and loving relationships, the first step is admitting that you are utterly powerless to love unconditionally. *Repita, por favor.* Unconditional love is unattainable in our own power.

The good news of the gospel is that in Jesus Christ we have the Good Physician. The world's preeminent heart cardiologist for our heart problems. And he offers the least expensive health care coverage in town. It's free, because he already paid the ultimate cost by his death on the cross and resurrection from the dead. If you don't know the seriousness of your heart condition, there's really no appreciation for the cure.

To discover the freedom found in loving unconditionally, we must first open ourselves up to the unconditional love of God. The depth of our need for God's unconditional love is seen in our inability to love without condition. We are wired to ask, seek, or demand, "What's in it for me?" Or in the words of the famous theologians ZZ Top, "Give me all your lovin' . . . give me all your lovin' . . . all your hugs and kisses too."

Gimme. Gimme. Gimme.

Yak bell love.

Condition upon condition upon condition.

God's asking you to turn in that old yak bell. Leave behind that clanky, clunky, monosyllabic conditional love. Follow a more excellent way. The way of the deepest desire of your heart that has already been paved for you. The apostle John tells us how God made a way for you and me: "This is love: not that we loved God, but that he loved us and sent his Son as an atoning sacrifice for our sins. Dear friends, since God so loved us, we also ought to love one another" (1 John 4:10). A better love story has never been written. Shakespeare can't come close.

God's unconditional love is love at all costs, because Jesus Christ has paid what you and I could never repay. By Christ's death on the cross and resurrection from the dead, God showed the full extent of his love for us. In doing so, he made a way for our impatience. Our unkindness. Our boasting and pride. Our anger and selfishness. Our

> If you want a loving marriage and loving relationships, the first step is admitting that you are utterly powerless to love unconditionally.

conditional love. Yes, our sin. God offers us for free what has cost you far too much for far too long. And his only condition is that we accept what we can't achieve or acquire on our own. Like Heidi's yak bell, it's a free gift, but with a lot more bells and whistles.

I know you might be feeling a little embarrassed. It's been said that God's unconditional love is the unbearable compliment. Not only is his love an unbearable compliment, it's downright embarrassing. We'd prefer to figure all this stuff out on our own, right? But try as we may, you and I can't create a symphony with a yak bell, Japanese gong, or cymbals from a marching band.

The good news is that there is the possibility of change and transformation. There is a more excellent way, and that's why I hope the good news of God's unconditional love is not old news for you. It is the greatest gift we get to open every morning of our lives. But for some people, good news becomes old news far too fast. That's why I sometimes wonder if boredom in marriage is tied to a "been there/done that" boredom with God.

I'm glad God offers us a more excellent way, because if he didn't, we'd really be trapped. Trapped in lifeless marriages. Trapped in ourselves. Trapped for eternity without him. Without the hope of restoration and transformation we'd be like a bunch of yaks lost in a snowstorm somewhere on the skirts of Everest. We'd never even make it back to the valleys where the majority of married life takes place. Oh, I know the valleys are messy places. Mundane, muddy lowlands where it's so easy to get choked by the haze and smog surrounding us. It's impossible to live there without inhaling some of it, but remember, God does his best work in the valley of everyday living.

Paul has a lot to show us on the road ahead. Let's go for a gander and see what we wear to hide from the very love that can transform our lives.

If you think yak bells are bad, wait until you slip on my dive hood.

CHAPTER FOUR

Dive Hood Desires

We walk around the valley wearing dive hoods, not realizing that the things closest to us are choking us, keeping us from the true life we were meant to live.

Heidi haggled for our yak bell in a noisy marketplace somewhere on the busy streets of Katmandu. We have another friend, however, another Heidi, who runs an international marketplace in her crowded garage in South Orange County. We call Heidi #2 the "eBay Queen." Most men hate to go shopping, but Heidi has now found a way to spend quality time together with her husband by wandering through online shopping malls. Is it possible to download a café mocha?

With a few mouse clicks, Heidi #2 has the world at her fingertips, a captive audience for the multitude of secondhand wares she hawks in bits and bytes in cyberspace. Her mass merchandise suppliers are not from Hong Kong or Singapore or other exotic locations across the world. No, Heidi frequents every thrift shop in South Orange County to find the best eBay booty. Short of a monster truck, anything Heidi can find, Heidi will sell online. Women's shoes. Children's clothing. Skateboard stickers. Surf wear. Makeup sample kits. You name it, Heidi has sold it. She once found a dozen or so vintage Holly Hobby dolls deep inside a cardboard box at a thrift store. Stole them all for ten bucks and then sold them on eBay for seventy dollars. Nice ROI?

So one day I'm thinking to myself, *How about that eBay?* Sounds simple enough. I work at home. I know how to use a computer. I like thrift shops. There are plenty of hard-to-find items in my local thrift stores, indigenous to California, that people all over America would love to have, right? Maybe a Nepalese man might be looking for the perfect American cowbell to give his wife as a birthday present. You know, one man's trash is another man's treasure.

A few days later, I stepped into the dank, dusty, dreary-looking St. Vincent de Paul's thrift store in San Juan Capistrano. I was confident. I was convinced that I was on to the Next Big Thing. I was going to bury Heidi with my eBay blitzkrieg.

I walked back and forth in the store, looking around, thinking, *What can I sell on eBay? What can I sell on eBay?* My eyes scanned the store. All of it looked like a bunch of junk, which it was.

But I was not to be frustrated. I remembered reading an article in the newspaper about a guy who made thousands of dollars selling vintage record albums online. I walked over to a box of old vinyl licorice and flipped through the records. Most of the albums were scratched, and the cardboard sleeves smelled like a leftover silverfish feast. I tested my marketing assumptions. *Would I buy my parents' Perry Como Christmas album? Is there still a market for Donny and Marie? Am I here to make money or waste my time?*

I kept a running conversation in my head. *Practical, I need something practical. What am I into? What do I like? Sports! That's what I can sell. That's what I know.* I dashed over to a silver trash can overflowing with sporting equipment. Dusty fishing poles with tangled lines and busted reels. Rusty golf clubs. I must confess, I had a secret hope of finding an extra Callaway or Taylor Made driver given away by a vengeful golf widow. Instead, I picked up an old wooden Jack Kramer tennis racket with a busted string. I remembered coveting one of those when I was a kid. I scrounged around the bin some more. I was not impressed with the Ping-Pong paddles and the tent poles minus the tent. "This is all just a bunch of junk," I muttered. As I surveyed the refuse before me, my enthusiasm waned. Heidi had made it sound so easy.

As I walked toward the front door, a rack of wet suits next to a bunch of old overcoats caught my eye. "Wet suits! That's it!" I exclaimed. What person living outside of California wouldn't want a great deal on a wet suit? How could I have been so blind?

Dollar signs in my eyes, I began pulling the wet suits off the rack. After a couple minutes of examining their condition, I was dismayed. My illusion of online entrepreneurship crashed like a personal computer. The wet suits were dated and tired looking; old seventies-era dive suits with lock-in beaver tails. On the verge of economic depression, I looked at the ground. *What's this?* I wondered. A slight hope fluttered inside my heart.

On the floor was a royal blue wet suit dive hood. I picked it up and looked inside. Men's large. Only five bucks. It was in good condition. Surely it would sell on eBay for at least twenty dollars. Maybe even thirty. What if I got a black Sharpie and forged Jacques Cousteau's name on it?

Scrounging around a bit more, I found another dive hood. Children's size. Hmm. The pickings were getting better and better. What dad in Minnetonka, Minnesota, wouldn't want to take his daughter ice-diving in the dead of winter? I could already envision my eBay product description: Deep Deals on Dad's and Daughter's Dive Hood.

Before paying for the high-quality, deep-discounted, destined-for-eBay dive hoods, I decided I'd better try on the men's large just to make sure it really was a men's large. Customer service is a big deal, and I didn't want any unhappy customers.

Standing next to the changing room, in full view of all the other store customers, who I was almost positive were eBay shopping sleuths like myself, I took a deep breath, stretched the dive hood as wide as I could, and pulled it over my head.

The dive hood fit like a glove. As tight as a surgical glove, that is, which was why the blood began to drain from my head. The hood was so tight that I felt like someone was shrink-wrapping my brain. I could see out of the eye portion of the hood, and nothing was preventing my mouth from taking in oxygen, but the neoprene material around my neck felt like a South American python squeezing my jugular. It was not my kind of neck massage.

Before I could even realize what I'd just done to myself, I was in the throes of a self-inflicted, dive hood choke hold. I wish I could say I was doing something really dangerous and adventurous like enduring the atmospheric pressure of diving two hundred feet underwater. No, I was at sea level about to pass out in a smelly thrift store.

I figured I had about thirty seconds left of consciousness. My brain intuitively knew that lack of oxygen leading to death is not a good thing, so I instantaneously placed my hands on the hood to rip it off. I grabbed the back of the mask and pulled as hard as I could.

I'm sure taking off a dive hood is a very easy task when the hood is wet, but my head and hair were as dry as a sun-drenched boat deck. After attempting to pull off my executioner's hood, the momentum of my thrust yanked me forward, almost sending me reeling into a rack of plus-size women's pants. I wobbled and staggered, trying to regain my balance. I began to get a bit woozy, kind of light-headed, like the guys on the top of Mt.

Everest. In a brief moment of clarity, seconds before I began to float toward a white light beckoning me, I thought to myself that this was going to be an awfully embarrassing way to die.

No one came to my rescue. I was sure the cashier was ready to call 911 to report a masked man trying to hold up the store. I attempted to pull the hood off a second time but failed again. I felt sympathy for the guy in the original *Alien* movie who lay on the spaceship's dining room table with a huge ball of alien goo stuck to his face.

In my asphyxiated state, exercising the universal sign of choking completely slipped my mind. So much for my CPR training. On the verge of suffocation by stupidity, my last attempt was do or die by dive hood. I dug my thumbs under the base of the hood, and with everything in me I wriggled through the tight, constrictive opening like a baby squeezing through the birth canal. I was only dilated to eight, but if I didn't push, I'd be a goner. The neoprene rubber tore at my hair, almost ripping off my scalp, and slowly peeled away from my head like a stubborn abalone being pried off a rock.

Pop!

I was finally free.

Sweating and exhausted, I gulped in voluminous amounts of air for my oxygen-starved lungs. And from the oxygen in my lungs came quiet laughter. A hearty belly laugh was out of the question — I'd already drawn enough attention to myself.

With large, sweaty blotches on my face, I humbly purchased my two dive hoods for ten bucks and sped home, eager to expend my eBay enthusiasm. Krista was skeptical, but Ellie thought the kid's dive hood was cool.

"Here, Ellie." I knelt on one knee. "Let's see how this fits. It's kid's size."

In retrospect, knowing what I know now, I would not have done at home what a semitrained professional could not accomplish in a thrift store. For my legal defense, I would argue that

I placed the dive hood on my daughter because of the severe hypoxic state I'd incurred back at the thrift store, resulting in the loss of several million brain cells. In testifying for the prosecution, Krista would probably argue that those several million brain cells hadn't existed *before* I walked into the thrift store.

I wriggled the hood over Ellie's head, and it fit—you guessed it—like a surgical glove. It took Ellie approximately 1.2 seconds to begin screaming and crying, "I can't breathe! I can't breathe! Get this thing off me! It's too tight!"

Krista yelled, "Get that thing off of her!"

Dumbstruck with dive hood déjà vu, I jumped into action and grabbed the hood, yanking Ellie's long hair in the process. She screamed at me as if I were pulling her head off, which I was. Her screams, from a cardiopulmonary point of view, were a good sign. At least she was getting air to her lungs. Several more ear-piercing screams and a couple tugs later, the dive hood released its death grip and allowed Ellie to come up for air. With squinting laser-beam eyes, she glared me into a fifty-gallon drum of guilt.

"I'm sorry, sweetie. I'm so sorry . . . Daddy didn't mean to hurt you!"

Six days later, I closed my first sale on eBay. After only two choking incidents and several hours posting the dive hood information online—not to mention how much time I spent going online to see how astronomically high my dive hoods were being bid up—my sale net the big bucks. Eight whopping dollars. I nearly choked my daughter and myself to death, and I lost two bucks. Talk about a cutthroat business venture.

I wonder what Paul would have auctioned on eBay?

Maybe Corinthian leather?

The city of Corinth didn't have e-commerce, but it was one of the strongest commercial centers of its day. It was a cosmopolitan city known for its flair and panache. It was the place to be. Business deals during the day. Late-night parties. Sexual pleasures served in the Temple of Aphrodite. Raging festivals of drunken-ness and orgies held throughout the city. All these decadent diver-sions and distractions kept the Corinthians busy and distracted from the voice of love calling out to offer a better way.

Paul's message to the Corinthians was deeply personal. He had serious work to do in explaining the nature of God's uncon-ditional love. Jesus Christ, whom Paul followed, was so unlike the erratic, temperamental gods of Greece and Rome. Not only did this Jesus rise from the grave after being dead for three days, but he gave a divine power, a transforming love, that could live in the hearts of those who chose to follow him.

But the Corinthians, like you and me, were easily distracted. They tried to pursue life apart from God's love, just like we try to pursue life apart from God's love. We walk around the valley wearing dive hoods, not realizing that the things closest to us are choking us, keeping us from the true life we were meant to live. And what we pursue apart from God's love will choke us like an eBay dive hood.

Let's read Paul's words again:

> If I speak in the tongues of men and of angels, but have not love, I am only a resounding gong or a clanging cymbal. If I have the gift of prophecy and can fathom all mysteries and all knowledge, and if I have a faith that can move mountains, but have not love, I am nothing. If I give all I possess to the poor and surrender my body to the flames, but have not love, I gain nothing.

We pursue many of the same things the Corinthians pur-sued. Knowledge. Education. Power. Wealth. Success. Status. Comfort. Luxury. Whatever their quantity, all of these good gifts come from God and present us with the opportunity to show God's love in action by sharing with others in need. God's gifts and his love were not meant to be retained but given away.

In the valley, however, we make the all-too-common error of confusing our blessings with a self-gratifying sense of entitlement and pride at our accomplishments. Apart from understanding and receiving all we have as extravagant gifts from God, we too often believe and behave like atheists. We deny the existence of God by extinguishing the free offer of his love. After all, we've worked hard for the conditional love of others. We are used to the terms and conditions of love. We've earned love as we know it. Throw in a little self-reliant pride, and I'll be darned if God pays my way.

Conditioned by all the conditional love we've experienced, we think the idea of receiving God's unconditional love as a free gift is just too good to be true. There are no free lunches or daily specials. We've skimmed over the fine print far too many times, and we're tired of being burned. There's always a condition. "Nothing is free," we mutter to ourselves as we sort through our cardboard box dreams and thrift store illusions of finding a better life out there. Instead of dropping the cumbersome load of the conditions we carry in our hearts, we are quick to perform all sorts of spiritual gymnastics, trying to earn what is already free.

And what we pursue, when we're not careful, ends up choking us.

I grew up in the San Gabriel Valley, and I can remember playing in the simmering August heat under a blanket of thick, hazy smog. After a day of riding my bike around the neighborhood and swimming in Charlie Morris's pool across the street, I'd lie in bed at night, careful to take slow, shallow

> Instead of dropping the cumbersome load of the conditions we carry in our hearts, we are quick to perform all sorts of spiritual gymnastics, trying to earn what is already free.

breaths. I couldn't breathe deep. One deep breath, and my lungs would burn from all the smog and chlorine I'd swallowed earlier in the day. On those hot August days, my lungs felt like I'd smoked four packs of Camels. The smog residue left in my lungs produced searing choking fits as I vowed to breathe a little less the next day. But smog or no smog, we do have to breathe in the valley, don't we?

> What is your life all about? In what you say and do, if you're not motivated by love, then who are you?

Regardless of the smoggy conditions of our hearts, God still woos us with his love. To help us understand the nature of God's unconditional love, Paul first guides us past aimless pursuits, those conditions of the heart that choke us. Whatever we do, whatever we know, whatever we have, or whatever we give up, if our core motivation isn't love, Paul essentially asks you and me, "What is your life all about? In what you say and do, if you're not motivated by love, then who are you?"

Paul serves it straight up. If we don't choose love and have love in our lives and marriages, we're just a bunch of clanging yak bells. No matter how forward-thinking and visionary we may be, no matter how smart we are, no matter how much faith we have, if we don't have love, we are nothing.

You may be an outstanding public speaker. A brilliant professor. A famous politician. A minister of a large church. Maybe nobody can craft a better message, a stronger sales presentation, or a more powerful sermon than you. But if you don't have love, your words are more hollow than the hole in a Lifesaver.

Maybe you're a CEO, CFO, or COO. A visionary business leader, someone with an incredible gift for forecasting what's happening on the economic horizon of the marketplace. But if you don't have love for the people you lead at the office and the family you lead at home, you are spiritually and relationally in the red.

Maybe you're a prophet in your own church. (Hopefully not self-appointed.) God has given you the incredible gifts of his Spirit: insight, discernment, wisdom, understanding. You can see what others can't see and hear what others don't hear. Your judgments are right on the nose. Your critiques hit the center of the bull's-eye. You smell the scent of sin in your congregation like a deer smells a hunter during hunting season. But without love, Jesus says you're no better than a whitewashed tomb. A self-righteous sepulcher filled with femurs and fibulas. No love. You prophet nothing.

Perhaps you're brilliant. The next John Nash with a beautiful mind. You can ponder and fathom the furthest reaches of physics. You can see and conceptualize the world of ideas, propositions, theories, and possibilities that others are not gifted to see. But do you love? Do you choose the most excellent way that creates transforming conditions in your marriage?

You have faith, you say. You have so much faith that you can move entire mountain ranges. You shuffle the deck and place the Rockies along the California coastline so no one can get to the beach. You anchor the Andes along the Mexican border to keep out the illegals who're trying to feed their families. And you place the Himalayas in front of anyone who tries to cut you off in traffic. That's a lot of faith. Did it move anyone closer to the love of God? Did you choose faith over love?

In God's eyes, it doesn't matter if you're a bleeding-heart liberal feeding the poor or a right-wing zealot surrendering your body to be burned for your beliefs—without love, good works and bold beliefs gain you nothing. Nada. Zip.

Eloquence without love. Prophecy without love. Knowledge without love. Faith without love. Sacrifice without love. You may be an incredible communicator, the smartest, future-forecasting, faith-building, sacrificial servant of humankind, but if you're heartless, God is not impressed. Without love, you and I miss the point of our whole existence.

Without love, we are nothing. We gain nothing.

Is it any wonder that so many marriages today are filled with identity crises? Without love, we have no idea who we are.

I believe the core problem of men and women struggling in their marriages is the absence of clear spiritual identity. We are broken people who don't know how to love very well, because we either don't know who we are or have forgotten who we are. Even as beloved children of God, we spend many of our days propping up a false sense of self, being and doing what others want us to be and do. We take our cues from the temperamental conditional love we've received, and we pay an inordinate amount of attention to who Madison Avenue is telling us to be. Many of us are spiritual adolescents struggling to grow up and grow in love. We want our freedom and independence, but we forget that our true freedom is found in remaining dependent children of God.

We live in a society that subscribes to the corporate illusion that life can be filled with meaning and purpose by filling the vacuum in our hearts with money and materialism, status and celebrity, drugs and alcohol, sex and any pleasure served to distract us from the nagging ache inside of us for a truly tender unconditional love. We desire better marriages. We want closer intimacy. We'd like to stop getting on each other's nerves, but on some days, it's all we can do to rip that dive hood off our heads to come up for air.

Jesus talked about the choked life. He knows of our incredible propensity to put on

> I believe the core problem of men and women struggling in their marriages is the absence of clear spiritual identity.

thrift store dive hoods. In the parable of the sower and the seed, he described a condition of the choked heart that is so common to life in the valley. "The one who received the seed that fell among the thorns is the man who hears the word, but the worries of this life and the deceitfulness of wealth choke it, making it unfruitful" (Matt. 13:22).

The worries of this life. The deceitfulness of wealth. Chokers. Dive hood desires.

Perhaps the most common ailment we suffer from in the valley is inhaling the smog of our own busyness. We choose busyness over love. The desires for all those other things — anything we try to fill our life and marriages with other than the love of God — get wrapped around our hearts and minds like a cheap thrift store dive hood. Author Michael Yaconelli characterized our busyness as a serious condition of our hearts:

> We are going as fast as we can, living life at a dizzying speed, and God is nowhere to be found. We're not rejecting God; we just don't have time for him. We've lost him in the blurred landscape as we rush to church. We don't struggle with the Bible, but the clock. It's not that we're too decadent; we're too busy. We don't feel guilty because of sin, but because we have no time for our spouses, our children, or our God. It's not sinning too much that's killing our souls, it's our schedule that's annihilating us. Most of us don't come home staggering drunk. Instead, we come home staggering tired, worn out, and exhausted because we live too fast.[1]

I love the simplicity of Jesus. An expert in the law, a real smart guy, stood up to test him. "Teacher," he asked, "which is the greatest commandment in the Law?" Get that . . . a teacher testing the Teacher. What is the greatest command to pursue? The best way? The most excellent way?

Jesus replied, "'Love the Lord your God with all your heart and with all your soul and with all your mind.' This is the first and greatest command. And the second is like it: 'Love your neighbor as yourself'" (Matt. 22:36–39).

These two commandments we looked at earlier are now circling back to us. If the conditions of our lives and marriages need to change, what must we choose above all else? The path to connecting with our spouses begins with loving God. It's the only road leading to unconditional love. To love your spouse unconditionally, you first have to know the Way. And you must know who you are as a child of God. Transforming change begins with this choice. It may not change your spouse, but loving the Lord God with all your heart, soul, mind, and strength, and loving your neighbor as yourself, will certainly change you. And God has to start with someone first, doesn't he?

Jesus loves you. He knows you. He's a heart doctor who also happens to operate a guide service. Let's follow and see who he says we are in him.

No thrift store experience required, but you may need a little wrestling experience.

That always comes in handy.

CHAPTER FIVE

Wrestling with Love

From the moment we're born to the day we die, our very existence hinges on hearing the voice of God whisper his unconditional yes into our hearts.

A idan is my youngest child. Four years old. There are many days when I wish I were Aidan's age. In fact, on some days, I think Aidan has a better idea of who he is than I do. I'd be a happy camper just to get a daily nap. I know God loves me, but as a child of God, I wrestle with love. His unconditional love.

Aidan doesn't wrestle with being a child of God. He doesn't even have a problem being a child of Joey and Krista. His needs are simple. Give him waffles for breakfast. Let him swing on his swing and play with Delaney down the street. After lunch, he'll do everything in his power not to take a nap, but once his soft blankie touches his cheek, he'll be out in minutes. He'll explore his inner artist and color on the wall when Mom or Dad isn't looking. Flannel jammies and a prayer at bedtime. And he'll wake up and do it all over again tomorrow.

Aidan isn't caught up in the hurries and hassles of living in the valley. Me, I'm all wrapped up in the business of everyday life. I wrestle with my choices and the limited nature of my conditional love. I wrestle with trying to allow God's love to change me from the inside out. I need a nap.

Not Aidan. He hates naps. He'd much rather be wrestling. Aidan has never seen WWF wrestling, but I'm convinced he has Hulk Hogan DNA. All Aidan cares about is wrestling. With me. The moment I walk through the door in the evening, Aidan runs at me, screaming, "Wet's wrustle!"

If I say no, not right now, Aidan collapses to the ground in a heap, as if every bone in his body has dissolved. Without his steady fix of wrestling, he's completely discombobulated. His grief is overwhelming. All-consuming. Akin to an Irish keener. I'm almost positive there are support groups for these kinds of problems.

All Aidan wants to do is wrestle with Dad. This is all that matters in the grand sphere of life when home is the center of the universe. To not have his wrestling need met in his time frame causes a major collision in his cosmos.

One night way past bedtime, I told Aidan it was too late to wrestle. As he protested with everything in him, I scooped him up over my shoulder, hauled him off to bed, and laid him on his dinosaur sheets.

"You don't wuv me," Aidan moaned from deep in his blankie.

"Yes, I do, Aidan," I said, trying to reassure. "You know I love you."

"No, you don't. You *don't* wuv me. You won't *wrustle* with me."

Aidan longed to hear his daddy say yes. Oh, how all of our hearts long to hear *yes*. From the moment we're born to the day

> Everything in us hungers for the yes of God.

we die, our very existence hinges on hearing the voice of God whisper his unconditional yes into our hearts. Everything in us hungers for the yes of God.

Knowing who you are as a child of God is the core of spiritual identity. Spiritual identity begins with responding to God's yes with your yes. Your voice responding to the Voice who calls you in love. It is the marriage of two wills as real as the day you stood at the altar and said yes to the one you love. And it is only by responding to the yes of God that we begin to understand what it means to say yes to the kind of unconditional love our spouses crave in the deepest part of who they are. Your yes to God enables you to keep saying yes to one another as you continue your journey together through the peaks and valleys of life.

Though it took Paul getting knocked off his horse on his journey to Damascus to hear God's tender voice of love, he discovered that God's unconditional love was an unconditional yes to who he was as a child of God. The love that transformed his life was no up-and-down, fifty-fifty, unstable, conditional kind of love. It was solid. Unchanging. Everlasting. Thoroughly dependable. Fault tolerant.

In writing to the Corinthians, Paul painted the yes of God in this light:

> But as surely as God is faithful, our message to you is not "Yes" and "No." For the Son of God, Jesus Christ, who was preached among you by me and Silas and Timothy, was not "Yes" and "No," but in him it has always been "Yes." For no matter how many promises God has made, they are "Yes" in Christ.
>
> *2 Corinthians 1:18–20*

In other words . . .

Whatever God has promised gets stamped with the Yes of Jesus. In him, this is what we preach and pray, the great Amen, God's Yes and our Yes together, gloriously evident. God affirms us, making us a sure thing in Christ, putting his Yes within us. By his Spirit he has stamped us with his eternal pledge — a sure beginning of what he is destined to complete.

MESSAGE

Remember playing the "No Means Yes and Yes Means No" game as a kid? It's a terrible game to play when you're trying not to get slugged. It's also a miserable spiritual game we play with God. Conditioned in our hearts by so much smog and sin in the valley, we forget or maybe haven't even heard that God's unconditional love is always yes. Yes always means yes. It's never no. It's never yes *and* no. It's never a tentative "We'll see . . ." like your parents used to say. There are no ifs, ands, or buts about God's love. God's love for you and me is always Y-E-S.

On nights when I give Aidan the thumbs-up signal for wrestling and after I have been thoroughly thrashed and trashed by my four pillow-smashing, chest-thumping, knee-dropping, fist-swinging, fanny-slapping, body-slamming, finger-fishhooks-in-the-mouth kids, I quit before I really get hurt. Krista absolutely loves my wrestling matches right before bedtime.

"All right," I bellow like a Marine drill sergeant. "Everybody to bed."

Then Krista gives me the drill. "You riled 'em up, you put 'em to bed."

"But I didn't start it," I object. That doesn't get me too far.

So I get everyone tucked in and prayed up. On many a night, I'll snuggle up to Aidan, who sleeps on a bottom bunk. His face is usually sweaty, radiating the heat generated by whomping on Dad. His warm breath caresses my cheeks as I place my face close to his.

I whisper, "Aidan, why do I love you?"

"Because I'm your son," he'll say in his little singsong voice.

I'll ask again, "Aidan, why do I love you?"

"Because I'm your son."

We'll do this three or four times until I sneak my hand under the covers and tickle his belly. He erupts into laughter, begging me to stop but loving it all the same. "Aidan, why do I love you?" He's now in full-blown silly mode. "Because you're a peanut butter face!"

Aidan knows who he is because he is loved. Aidan knows he is loved because he is a son. He knows connectedness. He knows relationship. He knows love. He knows someone has said yes to his yes.

At Jesus' baptism, right before the Spirit led Jesus into a wilderness ripe with tantalizing tests and temptation, the voice of his Father boomed out of heaven. "This is my Son, whom I love, with him I am well pleased." Jesus heard the yes of his Father. He heard his Father's voice calling out to his voice. The voice of the Father rooted Jesus in relationship—*this is my Son.* The voice of the Father provided the promise of unconditional love—*whom I love.* The voice of the Father affirmed his good pleasure in his Son—*with him I am well pleased.*

No conditions. No performance. No nos.

Only a yes. Only a relationship. Only the pleasure found in unconditional love. Just a dad loving his son.

We can have relationship without love, but we cannot have love without relationship. Connecting with your spouse begins with a deep and vital love relationship with God, because all love comes from God. Even though your spouse may be unloving or choose to love you with many terms and conditions, if you know who you are in God's love, you can choose a deeper love. A love like God loves. An unconditional love that keeps on loving in spite of someone acting unlovely, but a love that knows how to set limits.

Again, we've been inoculated with such confusing ideas about love that we have to remember unconditional love does not mean having no limits or healthy personal boundaries. As adults, we have the choice to love one another, and that choice implies that there are necessary conditions that must be present in order to nurture, develop, and keep the love alive. We can love unconditionally with limits and live within that paradox.

All relationships and all people must have the healthy conditions of honor and respect for one another in order for the relationship to grow and thrive. Because we live in a broken world, certain conditions must be met in order for a relationship to be sustained. Accepting abuse under the faulty thinking that you love your spouse unconditionally is not unconditional love. Remaining the target of someone else's sin—physical, emotional, or sexual abuse—for the sake of the relationship is not unconditional love. Sometimes the very best show of unconditional love is refusing to allow another person to hurt you any longer because the pain they are inflicting is detrimental for you and the relationship.

In counseling couples, I've discovered that a couple can be well aware of their issues and the necessary skills and tools and still not know how to connect to each other. What if a couple has been to multiple marriage counselors, tried all the techniques, read all the right relationship books, and still can't connect? It happens all the time. I am convinced, more than ever, that the core problem among husbands and wives today is the lack of a clear spiritual identity. We don't know how to love because we don't know who we are, and we don't know who we are because we have not first connected with God's unconditional love.

> Connecting with spouses begins with a deep and vital love relationship with God, because all love comes from God.

75

I am a big fan of solid biblical counseling. It's the continuing education most of us need, and it's far more useful for our relationships than hiding behind another MBA or doctorate. But in some cases, a lot of time and energy is focused on the mechanics of marriage practicality, and little emphasis is placed on a bold, robust marriage spirituality. Too often, we want a counselor's quick fix or a pastor's punch list of three points and a prayer to solve chronic problems. We don't want to wrestle with God; it'd be far easier to wiggle out of his grip by trying to fix our spouses instead of asking what really needs to change in *our* hearts.

I've met with many successful, friendly, attractive couples. People who look like they've arrived and have no need to travel any farther through the valley. And their marriages are headed for a train wreck. Listening to their problems, I've often wondered in compassionate amazement, *This person, this couple, has absolutely no idea who they are.*

These are exactly the kind of people Jesus loves to meet. People with problems. People who have no idea who they are but who refuse to keep pretending. People in pain. People who mess up, screw up, and who never seem to shut up. People whose hearts are broken from chronic head-on marriage collisions. People whose lists of conditions are longer than the San Andreas Fault and who know they don't know how to love. These are the people Jesus promises to help shape new lives forged in the speechless wonder of who they are becoming as children of God.

Don't believe me? Feel like you have to wear your Sunday best seven days a week? Not true. Jesus reserves his unconditional love for broken people filled with the very conditions that have created multiple messes in marriage.

Later Jesus and his disciples were at home having supper with a collection of disreputable guests. Unlikely as it seems, more than a few of them had become followers. The religion scholars and Pharisees saw him keeping this kind of company and lit into his disciples: "What kind of example is this, acting cozy with the riff-raff?"

Jesus, overhearing, shot back, "Who needs a doctor: the healthy or the sick? I'm here inviting the sin-sick, not the spiritually-fit."

Mark 2:15–17 MESSAGE

Jesus loves to meet us sin-sick strugglers in the valley, untangle all the thorns choking our hearts, and take us into his arms to whisper the most beautiful words we have ever heard: "I have loved you with an everlasting love; I have drawn you with loving-kindness" (Jer. 31:3).

Spiritual identity begins with wrestling with God and ends with resting in God's unconditional love. It's letting go of who you think you are or who others have said you are or who they think you should be and crying "Uncle!" to God by humbly accepting who he says you are. Spiritual identity is living with the loving knowledge that you are known by God and that you are loved with an everlasting love. Spiritual identity is understanding that it's not all about you. It's not all about your spouse. It's not all about your marriage. It's understanding that God is at the center of all life and that all of creation looks to him for ultimate meaning, purpose, and sustenance. John writes, "God is love. Whoever lives in love lives in God, and God in him," and "We love because he first loved us" (1 John 4:16, 19).

This is the truth of who we are. We are created to live in God

> Spiritual identity is living with the loving knowledge that you are known by God and that you are loved with an everlasting love.

and live in his love. The deepest, truest thing about us is that when we accept God's unconditional love and his offer of adoption to become his sons and daughters, we will discover the joy and security of knowing who we are in him. Only when we know who we are can we begin to love as God loves by giving our spouses what we have freely received from him.

We can follow the way of love and keep choosing the way of love if we know who we are. The direction Paul points us in begins with walking with God. Loving unconditionally begins with loving God. It does not begin with trying to be more lovable to your spouse. Your sheer willpower to try to love apart from God's love is an exercise in futility. If you and I could have everything our hearts desired in this world, and I mean everything—wealth, power, fame—everything Jesus was offered by Satan in the wilderness, our hearts would still ache for more. Even if we had all of our spouses' love, it still wouldn't be enough. Without God's love, we are left to wander around the wilderness. Can all of the counseling, tips, and techniques for communication, conflict resolution, parenting, managing finances—everything we read about in marriage books—really help us or our marriages if we don't possess a growing understanding of who we are?

When Paul wrote "Without love, I'm nothing," he was aiming at the very essence of how we see ourselves. He is not overstating the obvious: Without love, *I am nothing*. Without love, I cannot know who I am; I am void of true eternal purpose. Without love, I am nothing more than a self-absorbed shell of a person who exists for a few years on this earth seeking my own good. Others exist for what is beneficial to me, and if they require something of me, we can then seek to have a transactional symbiotic relationship, at least on a biological level, which puts us up a little higher than protozoa or spore samples.

This is the protozoa-esque problem plaguing so many marriages today. Loveless, transactional marriages. You give me what I want, and I'll give you what you want. As long as we both meet these mutual conditions, we can live in a relative state of peaceful coexistence. Existence, but not love. Relationship based on conditional transactions. Companionship, but no deep connection.

Too often, we look to one man or one woman to fulfill all of our hopes, dreams, and expectations, and then we are sorely disappointed when he or she does not measure up in helping us discover who we are and fulfilling our deepest need for belonging. Oh yes, we said we love one another unconditionally, but eventually the real relationship gives birth to a monster-size baby with a diaper full of smelly conditions. And this is good.

Our unrealistic expectations reveal and fuel our deeper need for something more. Something that only God can fill in the aching hole of our hearts. Sure, the valley provides plenty of distraction and entertainment to temporarily fill the ache, but the stuff we spend our lives wrestling for leaves us empty and exhausted, wanting more and more to fill this insatiable hunger. And if we listen closely to the hunger and thirst in our hearts, we will hear the loving voice of God calling us to him.

Paul's heart ached for the early Christians to know the depth of God's love for them. He wanted their identity, their sense of self, to be rooted in relationship with the Father. Transformed by the unconditional love of God, Paul prayed for our lives, our marriages, to be transformed as well.

> If we listen closely to the hunger and thirst in our hearts, we will hear the loving voice of God calling us to him.

For this reason I kneel before the Father, from whom his whole family in heaven and on earth derives its name. I pray that out of his glorious riches he may

79

strengthen you with power through his Spirit in your inner being, so that Christ may dwell in your hearts through faith. And I pray that you, being rooted and established in love, may have power, together with all the saints, to grasp how wide and long and high and deep is the love of Christ, and to know this love that surpasses knowledge—that you may be filled to the measure of all the fullness of God.

Ephesians 3:14–19

When we are rooted and established in God's love, Paul says that it's within our grasp to know the width, length, height, and depth of God's love shown to us in Christ—a love that surpasses all knowledge—so we can be filled with the fullness of God. Martin Luther King, Jr., said, "Love is the key that unlocks the door which leads to ultimate reality." When we love, we experience the ultimate reality of being close to the heart of God. When we love, we experience the fullness of God, becoming like him, reflecting who he is as we find ourselves in him. Discovering who we are in Christ is the journey of a lifetime, but that process begins with learning who God already says we are.

This is where Paul offers us great encouragement through the letters he wrote to all his friends in churches scattered throughout the world. Paul makes a great guide because he constantly encourages followers of Jesus to know and remember who they are.

Listen to the sense of security and confidence Paul speaks with as he explains who he is as a child of God and who we are as children of God. Paul knows who he is, but never without forgetting who he was. Remember, before Christ, Paul was a highly educated religious bigwig. He had position. People feared him. Without God, Paul had a clear sense of who he *thought* he was, but without love, in his own words, he was nothing.

To his friends in Galatia, Paul wrote about the death of the old Paul and the life of the new Paul: "I have been crucified with Christ and I no longer live, but Christ lives in me. The life I live in the body, I live by faith in the Son of God, who loved me and gave himself for me" (Gal. 2:20).

To his friends in Ephesus, Paul shared the richness of God's love and mercy shown to us in Jesus. We don't have to try to save ourselves in the valley or try to love through our own power, Paul tells us, because we have received the gift of love and life through faith in Christ.

> But because of his great love for us, God, who is rich in mercy, made us alive with Christ even when we were dead in trans-gressions—it is by grace you have been saved. . . . For it is by grace you have been saved, through faith—and this not from yourselves, it is the gift of God—not by works, so that no one can boast. For we are God's workmanship, created in Christ Jesus to do good works, which God prepared in advance for us to do.
>
> *Ephesians 2:4–5, 8–9*

To his friends in Rome, Paul explained how we can be freed from fear as children of God and how we can enjoy a wonderful relationship with a heavenly Father who loves us. Because Paul knows who he is, Paul can love and endure suffering at the same time.

> Because those who are led by the Spirit of God are sons of God. For you did not receive a spirit that makes you a slave again to fear, but you received the Spirit of sonship. And by him we cry "*Abba*, Father." [Or, "Daddy, wet's wrustle!"] The Spirit himself testifies with our spirit that we are God's children. Now if we are children, then we are heirs—heirs of God and co-heirs with Christ, if indeed we share in his sufferings in order that we may also share in his glory.
>
> *Romans 8:14–17*

81

To his friends in the town of Philippi, Paul disavowed everything he once thought important about himself. He admitted he was still in process, didn't have it all together, but he wasn't turning back.

> The very credentials these people are waving around as something special, I'm tearing up and throwing out with the trash—along with everything else I used to take credit for. And why? Because of Christ. Yes, all the things I once thought were so important are gone from my life. Compared to the high privilege of knowing Christ Jesus as my Master, firsthand, everything I once thought I had going for me is insignificant—dog dung. I've dumped it all in the trash so that I could embrace Christ and be embraced by him. . . . Friends, don't get me wrong: By no means do I count myself an expert in all of this, but I've got my eye on the goal, where God is beckoning us onward—to Jesus. I'm off and running, and I'm not turning back.
>
> *Philippians 3:7–8, 12–13* MESSAGE

When you know who you are, you can love with an authentic love. But before you choose to love, you must know you are chosen. All of this begins with saying yes to the voice of love calling out to you every day in the valley as you go to the grocery store, fight traffic, prepare your annual reports, make that sales call, draft another proposal, pick up the kids from school, fix the sink, coach your kid's baseball team, get the homework done, and wrestle with your kids way past bedtime.

> When you know who you are, you can love with an authentic love.

Turning from the wounding choke hold of sin and accepting the breath of life found in God's free unconditional love is what makes you a child of God, the freest kid in the whole wide world. It gives you the freedom and hope to love in a whole new way. This is the road that leads through the valley.

In the coming chapters, Paul gets down to the specific choices that characterize this most excellent way of love. As you'll see, he shows the difference between our confining conditional love and the freedom found in God's unconditional love. He pins down the very conditions you and I wrestle with in our marriages and shows us how the unconditional love of God is possible for everyone who chooses this most excellent way. It's a love you don't have to wrestle with, because God is for you and not against you. But if you do wrestle with love, that may be part of your journey, and that's okay. Love always wins, and as you go to bed tonight, see yourself standing in the winner's circle placed there by God himself.

And if you listen closely, you just may hear him whisper in your ear, *"Why do I love you?"*

Go ahead. Don't be embarrassed. Say it.

"Why do I love you?"

"Because I'm your son."

"Why do I love you?"

"Because I'm your daughter."

You can fall asleep safe in your Father's arms.

. . . With One (or More) Conditions

CHAPTER SIX

Pink Beads
of Patience

Growing in patience takes work, and the only way to do this is by showing up each day for practice.

I'm a very patient man. Except for when I'm impatient. Ask my wife. On my less than perfectly patient days when all the forces of humanity are marshalling against me like the D-Day invasion on Omaha beach, I ask the Lord to give me patience. And when I ask for patience, humbly and respectfully, I don't want to have to wait for it. I want patience right now.

I'm a very time-sensitive individual. I want the yes of God this instant. In my time frame. Pacific Standard Time. When patience doesn't come the moment I need it, I'm tempted to spiral into all sorts of spiritual confusion. Yes, you could say it puts me on the verge of a spiritual identity crisis. I have been raised the past twenty years in my faith with the understanding that if I need anything, anything at all, like a parking place near the front door of a restaurant when it's raining or a brand-new car like my neighbor's, all I have to do is ask in Jesus' name and it will be given to me. Not that I'm coveting the car or anything. Which is why asking for patience seems like such a small, itty-bitty thing. It's not like I'm asking to win the lottery. Not this very moment, at least.

If God is omnipresent (everywhere) and omniscient (all-knowing), why does it take him an eternity to get to me? All I need is a pittance of patience. And I'm not the only one in need of it. Krista needs me to have patience. My kids need me to have patience. When I reach the point of emotional exasperation, barely having the presence of mind to pray for patience, you know Krista and the kids are lining up right behind me, praying, "Lord, give him patience!"

One night in our kitchen a couple years ago, I lost my patience big time. It wasn't the pink plastic beads jamming our garbage disposal that made me lose it. Perhaps it had something to do with my building frustration over the previous few days of accidents, mishaps, and messes. Maybe my lack of patience stemmed from the three-inch rock I had to fish out of the toilet submerged amongst the toilet paper and downloaded software. Or maybe it was the three broken dishes smashed in one hour by one unnamed descendant, thus shattering the previously held O'Connor record by six minutes. Or maybe it was when I ran over a large Superball with my lawn mower, causing the mower to seize and smoke like it was ready to blow up in my face. So when a nameless, elusive somebody, somewhere in the vicinity of our kitchen, accidentally dropped a few pink plastic beads into the sink and promptly jammed the garbage disposal filled with leftover pasta, I'd about had it. Yes, I was a little miffed, but I had not lost my patience. Yet.

I'm not a plumber, and I know as much about garbage disposal repair as I do the manufacturing of pink plastic beads.

Like most people, I do not enjoy spending my evenings dismantling a garbage disposal designed to devour and macerate pink plastic beads. But what made me lose my patience, or as they say in West Texas, what "chapped me raw," was that one of my four innocent, honest children wouldn't 'fess up, own up, or take responsibility for our garbage disposal disability. For crying out loud, they didn't even try to rat on one another.

"Okay, who put the pink plastic beads in the garbage disposal?"

"I didn't."

"Wasn't me!"

"Me neither."

Three down, one to go.

I focused my interrogation on the last suspect of the Bead Bunch.

"Aidan, did you put the pink plastic beads in the garbage disposal?"

Perched in his white high chair and drooling over soggy Cheerios scattered across the tray, Aidan looked at me with his beady eyes as if to say, "And what if I did? You ain't getting nothing outta me."

He went back to his Cheerios. Babies get away with murder.

I turned my interrogation back to my three primary suspects. "Somebody had to have done it. Those little pink beads didn't just roll in there by themselves. There was no annual meeting of the Pink Plastic Bead Board. There was no vote to jam the O'Connor family garbage disposal, was there? Somebody's not telling the truth."

"I'm telling the truth," Janae said.

"I'm telling the truth," Ellie joined in.

"I'm telling the truth," Joseph chirped.

"Yeah," I snorted. "Well, somebody's not telling the truth. Somebody's lying."

"I'm not lying."

"I'm not lying."

"I'm not lying."

I briefly considered calling the FBI to inquire about the cost of purchasing a lie detector, but my kids have pretty sharp lawyers and I wasn't willing to spend the next few years in court. I also considered asking Krista in a nonchalant, nonthreatening way if *she* might have dropped the pink plastic beads in the garbage disposal. When all else fails, blame my wife, right? On second thought, I didn't want to get my head jammed down the garbage disposal. For my own safety, I dropped Krista from my list of suspects.

I was now facing a losing battle with the truth. I knew I had to reserve all my emotional energy for dismantling a piece of kitchen equipment that could take me weeks to put back together.

All of this truth-seeking tension was building up inside of me. The six of us were standing in the kitchen, and I was the only one feeling like a frustrated idiot with no answers and a busted garbage disposal.

Then I really lost it. As I was lying on the floor in an uncomfortable contortionist position, trying to dismantle the garbage disposal, my oldest daughter, Janae, reached into an upper cupboard and accidentally dropped a large box of Reynolds Wrap aluminum foil. The silver, serrated knife edge on the side of the box careened toward my head. Every primal fear I have about being decapitated surged through me in a split second. Have you ever nicked your finger on one of those Reynolds Wrap knives? Those puppies are sharp. Says right there on the box: Caution—sharp cutting edge. Narrowly missing the falling French guillotine blade, I ducked out of the way, and the box landed next to my head with a heavy thump.

"Janae!" I roared. "Watch what you're doing!"

Everyone stopped and looked at me. Praying for patience hadn't even entered my mind. All eyes were on me. Daddy just blew it. What's he going to do next? Janae broke into tears. I suddenly realized I had more than blown it. I got up off the floor, moved toward my daughter, and said in a quiet voice, "I'm sorry for yelling at you, sweetheart. I know dropping the box was just an accident. Would you forgive me?"

Janae nodded, wiping the tears from her eyes. A remarkable display of patience. She could have justifiably lashed back at me like I did to her, escalating the problem and making more distance between us.

Nobody has to tell us when we're being impatient. I know it. You know it. And everybody else knows it. We can't use the lame excuse "Well, that's just the way I am" and expect everyone around to march in goose-step formation behind us. When we're impatient, we can't deny or deflect our offensive defensive behavior by blaming the target of our impatience. Patience and impatience are equal, weight-bearing choices, but choosing the former over the latter is what leads to changing the conditions in our marriages.

When Paul writes about patience in the New Testament, his emphasis is not on patience with particular circumstances like pink beads stuck in the garbage disposal or rocks in the toilet. Paul's point is that we must be patient with people. In listing the very first quality of love in 1 Corinthians 13, Paul tells us that love is patient. The first step to changing the conditions in our

> When we're impatient, we can't deny or deflect our offensive defensive behavior by blaming the target of our impatience. Patience and impatience are equal, weight-bearing choices, but choosing the former over the latter is what leads to changing the conditions in our marriages.

marriages is to understand that patience is a condition we cannot live and love without. Patience toward our spouses is a practical, observable demonstration of our love. It is choosing to love in the same manner in which God loves. As we'll see in every condition of love that follows, Paul is helping us to understand the very nature and character of God. For everything Paul has to say about love, he is describing how God relates to us.

God is patient. He demonstrates his unconditional love toward us through patience with our flaws, our sins, our wanderings, and self-guided tours through the valley. Throughout our lives, God shows us his unlimited patience so that we might become more and more like him. He knows that spiritual transformation takes time, and his patience with us is absolutely necessary for us to grow in love and understanding of who he is making us to be.

Like God's unconditional love, patience must first be received from God, who demonstrates his patience with us. Patience is an indispensable condition for every marriage because it produces the perseverance we need to climb out of the valleys in order to reach the peaks. But patience, an authentic fruit of spiritual transformation, isn't conjured up by sheer willpower and self-determination. It begins with walking in step with God's Spirit, asking him to show us his perspective as we deal with people and problems. Being patient with our spouses has to be grounded in something more than a tacit acknowledgment that patience is a good idea because it helps people get along. Patience with others flows out of the spiritual perspective that God is patient with us.

This is Paul's perspective. What I love about his insights is

> The first step to changing the conditions in your marriage is to understand that patience is a condition you cannot live and love without.

that he doesn't try to hide his dirty laundry. He lets us know exactly how patient God has been with him. He admits he had no patience with the early Christians and that he, above all others, was "the worst of sinners." He doesn't throw out a bunch of lame excuses for his behavior, like, "Okay, so I cheat on my taxes a little. At least I don't cheat on my wife like the guy at work." No, Paul takes full responsibility for his actions and doesn't make any backdoor defenses by comparing himself to someone else. He says, "I am the worst sinner who ever walked the face of this planet. I'm as bad as you can get, but God has shown me unlimited patience." Listen to his own words.

> I thank Christ Jesus our Lord, who has given me strength, that he considered me faithful, appointing me to his service. Even though I was once a blasphemer and a persecutor and a violent man, I was shown mercy because I acted in ignorance and unbelief. The grace of our Lord was poured out on me abundantly, along with the faith and love that are in Christ Jesus.
>
> Here is a trustworthy saying that deserves full acceptance: Christ Jesus came into the world to save sinners — of whom I am the worst. But for that very reason I was shown mercy so that in me, the worst of sinners, Christ Jesus might display his unlimited patience as an example for those who would believe in him and receive eternal life.
>
> *1 Timothy 1:12–16*

Paul's horrific history as a murderer, blasphemer, and persecutor is given to us as an example of the unlimited patience of God. Paul was shown unlimited patience through God's unconditional love so that you and I would believe in Christ and be transformed. God desires for us to demonstrate his loving and patient character toward our spouses because he is loving and patient with us. When we are patient, we reflect God's love. When we're impatient and mean and rude, we reflect ourselves and the smallness of our hearts. This is why God places such a high premium on patience.

Just like putting on a fine watch or necklace, Paul tells us to clothe ourselves with patience (Col. 3:12). The way of love is marked by pink beads of patience. One at a time, bead after bead, the practice of patience strings together a beautiful necklace of love. We move forward through the valley and in our marriages when we practice patience. We fish for pink beads in the garbage disposal when we don't.

The Book of Proverbs has a lot to say about the privileges and perks that come with putting on pink beads of patience.

A patient man has great understanding,
  but a quick-tempered man displays folly (Prov. 14:29).

A hot-tempered man stirs up dissension,
  but a patient man calms a quarrel (Prov. 15:18).

Better a patient man than a warrior,
  a man who controls his temper than one who takes a city
  (Prov. 16:32).

A man's wisdom gives him patience; it is to his glory to overlook an offense (Prov. 19:11).

> Paul was shown unlimited patience through the unconditional love of God so that you and I would believe in Christ and be transformed by his amazing love.

How much folly, dissension, quarreling, loss of temper, and pointing out our spouses' offenses surface in our marriages because of a lack of patience? How much impatience flows from a lack of appreciation for the unlimited patience God has shown toward us? Flip that around and look at patience from this perspective: How would others describe you? How would you like to be known? As an impatient person or someone who displays great understanding? Do others look to you as the calmer of quarrels? Someone who is wise and who can control their temper? Whether you are the source of a conflict or the recipient of someone else's impatience, when you lose your patience, you are saying more about yourself than anything else.

> How much impatience flows from a lack of appreciation for the unlimited patience God has shown toward us?

The only problem is that patience isn't very sexy. When my wife and I are in a conflict, I don't know what it is, but she's not real interested in my sexiness. Patience makes me look quite boring. Almost frumpy. And I do not want to look frumpy. Frumpy is not manly. When I fail to follow through on something I promised to do for her, like picking the kids up from school, and she voices her complaint, what justice is there in not getting defensive? Why speak in a calm and controlled tone while embodying an aura of complete self-control? Where's the splash in that?

As I'm writing to you about the importance of patience, I'm holding a stack of loose-leaf papers from this chapter while standing at the end of the line in McDonald's with my four kids. This is real time. It's late afternoon on a Friday. I'm tired. There are three people in line ahead of me. I count twelve McDonald's employees and only one cashier, who can't decide whether or not to first bag fries or a Happy Meal toy. I am not a happy camper. I am seriously considering loading all of us back in the car, going through the drive through, ordering our meal, parking again, and bringing our food back inside so my kids can play in the Play Place. I'm ready to unload on the Mickey D's cashier. As to who is slower, it's a toss-up between him and the United Nations.

I glance at the customer comment box hanging on the wall, and I'm ready to write a scorching indictment on the poor customer service. I'm tempted to use my pen as a blowtorch, but I look at the cashier again. He's an eighteen-year-old kid. I suddenly realize I'm standing in a "patience line" and what I really need to order is patience. Super-size it. *God, please help me now before I throttle someone.*

God took my order right away. He knew all I needed was a pink bead of patience. I didn't need a whole necklace. Only a little gem would make all the difference in the world. Here's the perspective he provided. "Hey, Joey, you get to do what you love for a living. Well, why don't you jump over the counter and try working fast food? Some people *have* to work at McDonald's."

Thank you, Lord. That's exactly the perspective I needed.

Impatience fuels us with great power. Who hasn't wanted to unleash the power of impatience like Steve Martin did at the rental car checkout counter in *Planes, Trains and Automobiles*? Impatience energizes us. It fills us with awesome self-righteous power. There's only one wee problem. Impatience steamrolls the person we're being impatient with, squelching love and stifling any chance for creatively solving the problem.

So what does it take to be patient? A lot, especially if you struggle with impatience. Growing in patience takes work, and the only way to do this is by showing up each day for practice. Paul wrote to the Ephesians, "Be completely humble and gentle; be patient, bearing with one another in love" (Eph. 4:2). In our own power, we have a limited amount of patience that is filled with the terms and conditions we expect others to abide by in order for us to keep our cool. With the Holy Spirit, we have a power plant of patience available to us.

What is most amazing is that when we actually ask God for patience he is ready and willing to give it to us right now. It will usually begin with a tiny tap on the shoulder by the Holy Spirit reminding us how patient God has been with us. When we are on the verge of becoming a complainer to our spouses about the lack of customer service in our homes, all we have to do is step up to the counter and place our order. Ask for patience, and you'll discover free refills are included.

Marriage requires a constant refilling of patience. I hate to admit it, but I think Krista is far more patient with me than I am with her. When I am irritable or feeling overwhelmed with work, I am not much help when I point out in a less-than-understanding tone what needs to be done around the house instead of just getting in and being part of the solution. When I'm impatient with Krista, I fall under the category of what psychologists consider a "draining person." My impatience sucks Krista dry and does not endear me to her. On the other hand, when I am patient by trying to look at life from her perspective or exercising a measure of self-control with my words or tone of voice, I don't know what it is, but the day seems to go much better. Isn't it the same for you?

Patience is available, but it is a choice, and we can't underestimate how much work it really is to be patient. Like I said in the opening chapter, if you want to change the conditions of love in your marriage, you must be willing to work. And patience is the place to start. As you practice patience, you'll string a bunch of pink-beaded necklaces that your spouse and kids will learn to wear as well. It'll be a character-building craft for the whole family.

I never did discover who put those pink plastic beads in my garbage disposal.

Who knows . . . maybe God did. Maybe he knew I could use a bead or two.

Along with a little kindness.

> Ask for patience, and you'll discover free refills are included.

CHAPTER SEVEN

Choosing
to Be Kind

Disregard what the bumper sticker says. There are no random acts of kindness. Kindness is an intentional choice for people who want to follow the more excellent way of love.

There's a fascinating word play found in Luke's Gospel. Jesus is invited to a dinner party in the home of a Pharisee, a member of the local Sin Police. Jesus is the new kid on the block, and he's building quite a following. He's receiving more high fives, accolades, and attaboys than any religious leader since King David disco danced in the streets of Jerusalem. From what the Pharisees have seen so far, Jesus is the definitive crowd pleaser, which makes him Public Enemy #1 to the established religious rulers in Jerusalem and the surrounding outlet malls.

To put it lightly, Jesus has turned life in the valley upside down. Nobody wants to miss what he's going to do next. His teaching is refreshing and compelling, imbued with power and authority. Rumors spread from town to town that he is the promised Messiah. Word has it that Jesus is even a miracle worker. He's feeding people fish sandwiches by the thousands so they don't have to stand in line at Costco the day before Sabbath. The lame are doing Irish jigs. The deaf are telling family members to stop talking so loud. Blind people can find the morning paper on the driveway and actually read it. Dead children are playing hopscotch and jacks. Lepers are playing leapfrog with new limbs. Perhaps the wildest rumor circulating is that Jesus himself has actually claimed to be the Son of God. All of this amazing activity done in the name of God is enough to give the Pharisees a collective aneurysm.

So Jesus shows up for dinner. He's invited in by a Pharisee, a man by the name of Simon. Except for the flat-panel screen on the living room wall and satellite dish outside, Simon's home is modest. Unpretentious. Your basic Ikea décor. Though Jesus is a distinguished guest not lacking for social opportunities, Simon fails to greet him with the most basic of customary greetings. No welcome kiss. No washing of filthy feet covered in dust. No Oil of Olay anointed on his head. Surely the rest of Simon's guests, fellow Pharisees and high-society hobnobbers, had received the expected greeting from Simon.

Nonplussed, Jesus sits down. The room is crowded with guests. Everybody who's somebody is in the house. It's a good vibe. The chicken kabob appetizers are terrific. Everyone's waiting to see what Jesus is going to do tonight. Wherever he goes, he's either thrown out of town or somebody throws him a party. His life has little subtlety. Tonight it's party time.

As cocktail glasses tinkle and the guests make small talk, nobody seems to notice a woman slink through the front door and make her way to the center of the room. But when she gets to the feet of Jesus, my oh my . . . what do we have here?

It's *that* woman. Who let her in? Her reputation around this town is longer than the forty years Moses spent in the desert.

And would you look at what she's wearing? For goodness sake, put something on or take it down the street to the corner bar. Snickers and cackles zip through the air like glowing sparks in a nearby fire. All eyes are on Jesus. Jesus' eyes are fixated on the tramp before him. She's now kneeling and weeping at his feet.

A mixture of scorn and embarrassment seethes through the crowd. More than a few thought-bubbles are popping out above the party goers' heads: *Aw, give it a rest, woman! Stop your sniffling, would ya? Leave Jesus alone. The guy's been working hard all day long and now you show up. Get your filthy hands off the Messiah! You made your bed, many beds, now sleep in it!*

Muddy rivulets snake down Jesus' feet. The woman's weeping turns into uncontrollable sobbing. She's a pathetic mess of clothing and hair, her face shivering with overwhelming grief. Dropping on the Savior's feet, the woman's crystal tears turn brown, baptizing the grime on God. She towels Jesus' feet with her hair, the dark locks absorbent enough for an adequate foot washing.

Oh no, more than a few are thinking. *Now she's kissing his feet!* The room is silent. Shocked faces wonder what's next. The woman reaches for a small jar she brought with her, an alabaster jar to be exact. After she breaks it open, an intoxicating scent of perfume permeates the air. A little like White Diamonds, but different. Expensive nonetheless. She pours the perfume on Jesus' feet. Jesus smiles.

Meanwhile, Simon's in the kitchen making sure the cook doesn't put too much garlic in the lamb. He's had terrible heartburn lately, and if he's footing the bill by having so many people over for dinner, he wants to make sure it's a meal he can enjoy. *That's funny,* Simon thinks. *Why's it suddenly so quiet?* He throws a few leeks in the pot and exits the kitchen, wondering what's going on.

Simon walks into the living room, the scene before him catching him completely off guard. On the floor, in the middle of his house surrounded by dozens of important guests, is the lowest life form of a call girl he's ever seen. Who let her in here? Simon sniffs the air and takes in a whiff of perfume. Smells like White Diamonds. Like his mother used to wear. Simon looks at the woman and growls behind his teeth. She's prostrate, sobbing at the feet of Jesus. *Oh, this is great . . . just great,* Simon thinks to himself. *The guys at the office are never gonna let me forget this one!*

Simon is furious and embarrassed for himself and his reputation. The thought of being pronounced "unclean" for having a harlot in his home is enough to send him reeling. A thought crosses his mind. *Maybe I can save face? If Jesus really is the kind of prophet everyone else says he is, he would know what kind of woman this is. If I were him, I'd put this prostitute in her place and out of my place the second she walked through the door!*

Jesus touches the woman on the shoulder and looks up at Simon. "Simon, I've got a story for you."

Simon is startled. All eyes are on him. He swallows a lump in his throat the size of a lemon and responds to Jesus. "Tell me the story, Teacher."

"Two men were in debt to a banker. One owed five hundred silver pieces, the other fifty. Neither of them could pay up, and so the banker canceled both debts. Which of the two would be more grateful?"

Simon answers, "I suppose the one who was forgiven the most."

"That's right," says Jesus. "Do you see this woman? I came to your home; you provided no water for my feet, but she rained tears on them and dried them with her hair. You gave me no greeting, but from the time I arrived she hasn't quit kissing my feet. You provided nothing for freshening up, but she has soothed my feet with perfume. Impressive, isn't it? She was forgiven many, many sins, and so she is very, very grateful. If the forgiveness is minimal, the gratitude is minimal."

Then Jesus speaks to her. "I forgive your sins."

That set the dinner guests talking behind his back. "Who does he think he is, forgiving sins?"

Jesus ignores them and says to the woman, "Your faith has saved you. Go in peace" (Luke 7:41–50 MESSAGE).

The woman at Jesus' feet stands up. She wipes the tears from her eyes and in a strange way looks remarkably refreshed. She heads for the door, walking past the dumbstruck guests, but not in a hurry. Simon opens the door with a scowl on his face, and the woman leaves, but not before flashing him a smile of undeniable freedom. Simon storms into the kitchen, tastes the lamb, and yells at the cook. Too much garlic.

In this wonderful story, Simon the Pharisee ruminates whether or not Jesus knows what kind of woman lies at his feet. Of course, Jesus knows what kind of woman she is. She's a woman of the night. A hooker. A card-carrying call girl with a little black book the size of the yellow pages. Jesus knows exactly what kind of woman she is, but what Jesus shows her is that his love is kind.

Simon sneered at the prostitute and her outrageous demonstration of humility with a judgmental and critical contempt. He was righteous. A ceremonial Mr. Clean. And this woman stormed into his home. Uninvited. Unwelcomed. And worst of all, unclean as pork served on the Sabbath. Simon's judgment of this weeping woman placed him squarely in Jesus' bull's-eye for everyone in attendance to learn a lesson in kindness. Through warmth and compassion, Jesus lavishes upon this woman the undeserved depths of his love. Just as she anoints Jesus' feet with expensive perfume, Jesus bathes the woman with the riches of his kindness.

What would happen if you and I bathed our marriages in the kindness of Christ?

If there are three dangerous practices that unravel the transforming power of kindness in marriage, they are criticism, contempt, and condemnation. All examples of conditional love. The three Cs unleash untold amounts of insecurity, defensiveness, revulsion, anxiety, uncertainty, pain, and frustration. There is nothing more damaging for a marriage than for a husband or wife to practice the all-too-familiar verbal martial arts of criticism, contempt, and condemnation.

We karate chop what our wife is wearing or how her hair looks.

We kung fu kick our husband for how little money he makes.

We backhand our beloved with demeaning words about how much she weighs.

We tae kwon do our husbands with nagging and whining.

Taking one another to the mat, we are black belts in our ninja warfare of words. Sooner or later, one of us gets tired of playing this game and is ready to call it quits. Cumulative criticism, cumulative contempt, and cumulative condemnation get old real quick, creating a destructive cycle of pain that undermines the vows we made to cherish and love one another.

Paul understood what it meant to battle criticism and unkind words. Having firsthand knowledge of what it was like to be an undeserving recipient of God's kindness, Paul warned the church in Rome about having a judgmental, critical, and conditional attitude toward others.

You, therefore, have no excuse, you who pass judgment on someone else, for at whatever point you judge the other, you are condemning yourself, because you who pass judgment do the same things. Now we know that God's judgment against those who do such things is based on truth. So when you, a mere

If there are three dangerous practices that unravel the transforming power of kindness in marriage, they are criticism, contempt, and condemnation. All examples of conditional love.

man, pass judgment on them and yet do the same things, do you think you will escape God's judgment? Or do you show contempt for the riches of his kindness, tolerance and patience, not realizing that God's kindness leads you toward repentance?

Romans 2:1–4

There's that patience word again. In his unconditional love for us, God not only exercises patience with us, he also shows us the riches of his kindness. And it is God's kindness, Paul says, that leads us to repentance, which means we are to stop and turn from a life of sin, judgment, and contempt for other sinners like ourselves. When we demonstrate an unkind, judgmental attitude toward people, we are trying to dethrone God and bump him off the judgment seat. You be the judge, but I don't think God takes too kindly to this type of behavior.

When we critique our spouses, we are offering unsolicited advice with a mean spirit. We may say the words "I love you unconditionally," but if we're carrying criticism, contempt, or condemnation in our back pocket, we are straddling the fence of a very precarious conditional love.

That said, we all use unkind words. No marriage is immune from them, because, like the woman at Jesus' feet, we are all sinners with forked tongues. Of course, we don't really have forked tongues. This is a mere metaphor. Anyway, there's one side of our tongues that really does love our spouses, wants the best for our marriages, and uses kind words to spread a fragrance of love and affection throughout our homes. There's the other side of our tongues that is nasty as a cunning cobra ready to spit poison at the slightest provocation. Cross me and I'll spit in your eye. Notice again, I am using metaphor, a literary device. If I ever did that to Krista, she'd poke my eye out.

In his kindness, Jesus is willing to touch all kinds of people. That includes you and me. Your marriage and mine. Despite how unkind and critical we can be, God is kind to us, and in his unconditional love, he draws us to himself even when we act most unlovable. Jeremiah, the Old Testament prophet who had a heap of trouble with the nation of Israel, said, "The LORD appeared to us in the past, saying: 'I have loved you with an everlasting love; I have drawn you with loving-kindness. I will build you up again and you will be rebuilt'" (Jer. 31:3).

Unkindness is what tears marriages down, and through God's promise to build us up, kindness is what rebuilds them. No marriage can survive without the riches stored up in simple deeds of kindness. Disregard what the bumper sticker says. There are no random acts of kindness. Kindness is an intentional choice for people who want to follow the more excellent way of love. There is nothing haphazard about being kind. It's a direct result and a verifiable proof of a life transformed by the unconditional love of God.

Spiritual transformation, this process of being rebuilt from the inside out to become more and more like Christ, is possible only if we are keenly aware of God's kindness in our lives. When Paul wrote to his friend Titus, he looked back at what a foolish life he had lived. A life filled with malice, envy, and hatred. Reflecting on who he was before he encountered Christ, Paul wrote, "But when the kindness and love of God our Savior appeared, he saved us, not because of righteous things we had done, but because of his mercy" (Titus 3:4–5).

God's mercy is the practice of his kindness. God draws us to himself with loving-kindness. Because he is merciful, God desires us to have a deeper relationship with him. Because he is loving, he exercises

> Disregard what the bumper sticker says. There are no random acts of kindness. Kindness is an intentional choice for people who want to follow the more excellent way of love.

his patience and kindness to us. Because he is kind, God desires to show us all of who he is so that we can become all he has made us to be. Learning to become gentler, kinder people is part of this process.

This is what I love about my wife. Above all else, Krista is kind. Her love is best demonstrated by her kindness (and patience!) with me and the kids. Maybe it's because she's got this "K" alliteration thing going, but Krista's kindness is what makes her a very wealthy person. She has a broad cross section of friendships and significant relationships because she treats people with kindness, dignity, and respect. She treats people like Jesus does.

This is the type of wealth Paul is pointing us to by showing us the more excellent way of love in our relationships. Paul was serious when he spoke of the riches of God's kindness, because people who are kind have far more wealth than people with piles of money.

> Paul was serious when he spoke of the riches of God's kindness, because people who are kind have far more wealth than people with piles of money.

True wealth in the valley is earned through deliberate acts of kindness that build up your spouse, instead of resorting to criticism and judgment. And kindness is a sure way to woo a wounded heart. Regardless of what unkind thing you've done or said this past week, it is never too late to show kindness. God is love, and love is kind. And God makes his loving-kindness available to you so you can pour out the fragrance of his love wherever you go.

Be kind and your spouse will swear you smell different.

And your kindness will be the envy of others.

CHAPTER EIGHT

The Green-Eyed Monster of Envy

Envy is an equal-opportunity error of the heart. It's the all-seeing eye of spiritual emptiness. It's our heart searching for a home in someone else's stuff or success.

Christmas is a terrible time for the emergence of envy. It's one of those mountain peak times, a time to emerge out of the valley and get some perspective on the past twelve months. It's a time of celebrating and feasting, a time for reflecting on how far we've traveled in the valley, and a time for focusing on what matters most. It's a time when I want to look back and be thankful for all the blessings I've received as I put the final touches on my newly revised Christmas list.

Nothing ruins the Christmas season more than the gimme-gimme guilty feeling emanating from envy. Envy during the holidays is a sure recipe for a second-story swan dive into a guilt bath thick as eggnog. And I can do without the extra calories. If we could break sin down into different food groups at Christmas time, envy is the spiritual equivalent of fruitcake.

My Christmas story begins with Krista and me receiving an invitation to a Christmas party from one of the ladies on her tennis team. After not having played since college (having four kids kind of does that), Krista recently began playing on a doubles team with her sister Lisa. Since competition is at the core of envy, tennis is about as good a sport as any to covet to the death.

The hostess of the party, Krista told me, was a very nice lady both on and off the court. She wasn't like one of those nasty tennis lady tyrants who get all persnickety when someone makes a bad call. Krista assured me we wouldn't stay long — I didn't want all the other husbands getting jealous as Krista showed me off, her trophy husband.

This was also the lady, Krista said, with the diamonds.

Oh, that lady. This will be interesting.

The previous month, Krista had regaled me with stories of conversations with ladies at the club. Some women liked to talk about their kids. Some talked about their crafts and hobbies. Others talked about their careers or things they liked to do. This lady, the nice one, we'll call her Debbie, liked to talk about her diamonds.

"You should see the size of this lady's rocks," Krista told me one day. Not that I felt any pressure or anything. Not that the average eye needed the Hubble space telescope to see the diamond I bought Krista for our wedding. Not that I was envious or jealous or the least bit threatened that my wife was going on and on about Debbie's diamonds.

"Okay, can we talk about something else now?"

The night of the party, I was tempted to mount a small magnifying glass on Krista's left ring finger to subtly enlarge her wedding ring and thus increase the "wow factor" of her diamond by ten times. I dismissed this idea after realizing the duct tape would be a dead giveaway. Super glue was out of the question, so I'd just have to suck it up and let the social chips fall where they may. It never occurred to me that Wal-Mart was on the way to their home. I missed a perfect opportunity to load up on a bundle of cubic zirconiums before the party.

Krista and I were one of the first couples to arrive at the party. It was a brand-new Mediterranean home in a large cul-de-sac in a new subdivision, not too far from our twenty-year-old housing tract. We rang the front doorbell and smiled at each other. Krista looked pretty. She was wearing a long black dress and a string of pearls I'd given her before our wedding day. Pearls, not diamonds. My mom paid for them. They were kinda from me. In a conduit sort of way.

Before the front door swung open, in a split-second daydream, I visualized the door opening and thousands upon thousands of sparkling diamonds pouring out, diamonds of all shapes and sizes, leaving Krista and me buried waist deep in the glittering gems. *You are a twisted individual,* I thought to myself as the front door opened.

"Hi, there! Welcome, I'm so glad you could make it," a friendly woman greeted us. *We're at the right house,* I thought. The woman was wearing diamond earrings the size of ice cubes. Huge, mesmerizing diamonds. I almost got lost in a cobralike trance.

"Hi, Debbie, this is my husband, Joey," Krista said as I pulled out a pair of sunglasses to protect my eyes from the glare. I gave a cordial hello, trying my best to make eye contact, but her diamonds provoked in me a deep need to gawk. Debbie also was wearing a beautiful diamond necklace and a large diamond ring. Not that I was looking for additional accessories or anything.

We entered the home, which was beautiful and immaculate because company was coming over. I don't know about you, but company is our best motivator for cleaning up. I get so tired of our kids leaving their diamonds all over the place.

Marquise diamonds left under the couch. Pear diamonds trash-
ing up the back porch. Oval diamonds littering the hallways.
And all those bothersome round diamonds strewn across the
tile floor. I am so sick and tired of having to sweep up all the
diamonds before company comes over that I've warned our
kids that if it happens again, there will be no Rolexes on their
next birthday. I'm serious.

Krista and I sauntered through Debbie's home, making our
way past the billiard room with its red-painted walls. We entered
the kitchen, the decor modern with the latest in high-end, expensive kitchen appliances. The granite counters were covered
with hot chafing dishes. Another long granite counter was filled
with plate upon plate of Christmas goodies. The room next to the
kitchen had plush custom couches, large, glowing candles, and
a big, big, big television screen. Do you ever have the feeling of
liking your own kitchen and your own home, but then you walk
into some stranger's kitchen and say to yourself, "This! This is
the kitchen I really want!" Not that I was envious or anything.

I walked outside to the pool area, where the drinks were
being served. I met Debbie's husband, who was standing behind
a large stone bar under a permanently affixed heating lamp.
He wasn't wearing any diamonds, not that I was checking him
out or anything, but the incredible backyard landscaping filled
with pine trees, custom cement hardscape, and soft, comfortable patio furniture nearly set me over the edge.

Enough, I admitted to myself and to God, starting a quick
conversation with him. You have blessed me in many, many
ways, but right now, I confess that I am coveting this house,
this home, and everything in it. Including the diamonds!

Christmas music played on the outdoor speakers as I held my
Perrier and felt really crummy about coveting at Christmastime.
Not that I should feel good about envy or jealousy or coveting
at any other time of the year, but this was different. I'm usually
pretty grateful for what I have and not prone to being envious

of what others have. Sure, I could buy more, spend more, and rack up a ton of debt (it is the American way, you know) to try to keep up with the Joneses. But why?

Seeing this beautiful home and tapping a mental calculator in my head, making a rough estimate of how much this beautiful backyard must have cost, sadly reminded me of two friends who got divorced a couple years ago. For years, Don and Teri had struggled financially as Don tried to find a right fit in the industry in which he worked. Both had fun personalities and were active in church and different ministry endeavors. Our kids played together, and every so often we'd get together for breakfast.

One day after church, we went over to their home for bagels, and Don showed me some of the remodel changes he'd been working on in the kitchen and backyard. New doors. New stone patio. New windows. New fireplace. New Jacuzzi. The remodel was going well, and it certainly looked nice, but in my mind I wondered how they were going to pay for it. I knew they'd been struggling financially, but I kept my thoughts to myself, reasoning that things must be going okay after all and that it was none of my business. All I knew was my own experience with financial struggles. Having worked for a number of years on my own, I knew firsthand how much pressure financial struggle places on a marriage. When times were really thin, there were no extras. No perks. No remodels. No diamonds. Not that Krista has any more diamonds now than she did then.

As we sat down to eat our bagels, Don casually remarked, "Yeah, we just took a second out on our home to pay for it all. It's only twenty thousand, and we can pay it off over thirty years. That's what everybody does!"

I almost choked on my cinnamon raisin bagel. "That's what everybody does," I said in a loud, incredulous voice. Don laughed it off, and we went back to eating our bagels, but not before I thought about how this nice remodel would amortize over thirty years. Ouch! Two years later, Don and Teri divorced. Not that the remodel caused the divorce. People divorce people; remodels don't.

After their divorce, I couldn't help but wonder if the remodel was just a distraction to a marriage already headed in the wrong direction. What if Don and Teri had been able to look at some of the complicated issues creeping into their marriage from a new perspective? What if more time and money had gone into remodeling their marriage? What influence, if any, had envy played in the decision to rack up twenty thousand dollars in debt plus interest at a time when they were struggling financially? What had influenced Don and Teri's thinking, or more important, their hearts, to make such a significant decision because "that's what everybody else does"?

Whatever the reasons for Don and Teri's divorce, what's really sad about Don's comment is that their spending habits aren't unusual or uncommon. There is more truth than fiction to Don's words, and they reflect the reality that if "everybody" is up to their eyeballs in consumer debt, then "everybody" must have their eyes on everyone else.

> Envy can turn you and me as green as an alien and make our hearts as cold as Planet Pluto. Just like the condition of my heart when I had my eyes on Debbie's diamonds. And kitchen. And backyard. And big, big, big television.

Pure old-fashioned envy.

Envy can turn you and me as green as an alien and make our hearts as cold as Planet Pluto. Just like the condition of my heart when I had my eyes on Debbie's diamonds. And kitchen. And backyard. And big, big, big television.

Envy is an equal-opportunity error of the heart. It's the all-seeing eye of spiritual emptiness. It's our hearts searching for a home in someone else's stuff or success. And it diminishes another's success and reveals the shadowed corners of our hearts that are hungry for what has been earned by another.

Shakespeare called envy "that green-eyed monster."

Teddy Roosevelt said that "the vice of envy is always a confession of inferiority."

John Dryden wrote that "jealousy is the jaundice of the soul."

You know what Paul said: *Love does not envy.*

A loveless, green-eyed monster making a confession of inferiority from the yellow-bellied center of its soul. Strong words. If David Letterman ever spoke for God's Top 10, envy would be first on his list. God was quite specific when he wrote about envy. He didn't just say, "You shall not covet." Detailed God that he is, he had his anticovet checklist in hand when he said, "You shall not covet your neighbor's house. You shall not covet your neighbor's wife, or his manservant or maidservant, his ox or donkey, or anything that belongs to your neighbor."

That small, conditional word "anything" includes just about everything.

The problem with "coveting" or "envy" is that envy has its eyes on everyone.

Everyone but God.

It is coveting that creates all the wrong kinds of conditions in our marriages. Coveting reduces unconditional love, a love that freely gives and receives, to a gimme-gimme conditional kind of love. Envy in modern marriages can be so deeply rooted and so insidiously subtle that we don't even notice the power it holds in our lives. Envy influences our decision-making, career choices, credit card and home loan balances, whom we socialize with, how much time we spend with our kids, and how we spend the rest of our time. If the grass is always greener on the other side, then whatever the "green grass" is—money, possessions, the perfect body, success, or the latest Hummer SUV—will never be found. Hording possessions or status will always leave our souls void and empty of true eternal purpose.

> What couple isn't prone to envying one another's time? How many conflicts in marriage are centered around the clock and how much free time we get to pursue our pleasures?

Envy rears its ugly head in all sorts of ways. It's closely tied to the expectations we bring with us into marriage, but how often are we honest about what our expectations really are? We expect our spouses to provide us with a nice home. Material pleasures. A vacation every year. A nice, fat lump sum to sit on during retirement.

If we're not envying the possessions, success, or accomplishments of our neighbors, we can often turn our envy inward in our marriages by envying one another. What couple isn't prone to envying one another's time? How many conflicts in marriage are centered around the clock and how much free time we get to pursue our pleasures?

"Honey, this weekend I'm going _____"
   (fill in the blank).

"Oh no, you're not! I've had the kids all week long and now it's your turn."

"You went out with your girlfriends, so now it's my turn to go out with the guys."

"You never spend any time with me or the kids because you
  work so much."

"The reason I work so much is to pay for everything you
  and the kids want to do."

Sound familiar?

We rob our families of our presence in pursuit of the stuff we
think will bring us ultimate satisfaction. I sincerely believe that
envy is at the heart of many marriage struggles because in the crazy
pursuit of achieving success in the valley, we sacrifice so many
things to get what we can never keep. We sacrifice our marriages.
Our children. Our lives. All on the unsatisfying altar of success. As
someone once said, "I climbed the ladder of success only to discover
at the very top that it was leaning against the wrong wall."

In one way or another, we all battle that green-eyed monster
in our hearts because we all envy. Here in America, we're surrounded by creature comforts, and it's next to impossible to
live in the valley of everyday life without experiencing envy.
We think that success and the stuff that comes with it will
bring us significance.

If the apostle James was a marriage counselor, he just might
have said to us:

> Where do you think all these appalling wars and quarrels come
> from? Do you think they just happen? Think again. They come
> about because you want your own way, and fight for it deep
> inside yourselves. You lust for what you don't have and are
> willing to kill to get it. You want what isn't yours and will risk
> violence to get your hands on it.
>
> You wouldn't think of just asking God for it, would you? And
> why not? Because you know you'd be asking for what you have no
> right to. You're spoiled children, each wanting your own way.
>
> You're cheating on God. If all you want is your own way,
> flirting with the world every chance you get, you end up enemies
> of God and his way. And do you suppose God doesn't care?

The proverb has it that "he's a fiercely jealous lover." And what he gives in love is far better than anything else you'll find. It's common knowledge that "God goes against the willful proud; God gives grace to the willing humble."

So let God work his will in you. Yell a loud no to the Devil and watch him scamper. Say a quiet yes to God and he'll be there in no time.

James 4:1–7 MESSAGE

When Paul wrote "Love does not envy," he was speaking to a materialistic Corinthian culture whose eyes purveyed the finest goods and products from all over the world. Corinth was a Pier 1 Imports of sorts, and the Corinthian people had ample opportunity to see and envy the latest in designer fashion and textiles, custom home furnishings, exotic foods, and leather goods. Paul knew the people of the Corinthian church wrestled with envy, just as God knows that you and I wrestle with this green-eyed monster. Paul also knew a more excellent way.

Want to behead that green-eyed monster? Love is the only way to lop it off. Excising envy from your marriage means pursuing love as the most excellent way rather than envying what you can't or don't have. Love does not envy anything or anyone, because love is content.

Contentment and gratefulness are the greatest antidotes to the poison of envy that jaundices our souls. You see, here in the valley, you and I were never meant to arrive. We weren't made to wear diamonds on the soles of our shoes. The Bible says we are strangers in this land. We're just passing through. We were not meant to acquire and possess but to love and give. Sure, we all have our possessions, and there's nothing wrong with owning or liking nice stuff, but our stuff is never meant to possess us. Our hearts are made to possess the love of God. Contentment and gratefulness are the only cures for the cravings that lead us to envy. Choosing contentment can lead you and your spouse to making lifestyle decisions that fit a transformed heart and life. And budget.

When you and I stop to think about it, we both have a lot to be grateful for. The next time we're feeling the slightest twinge of envy, why don't we both sit down and come up with a long list of everything we do have instead of looking at what we don't have? And while we're at it, why don't we also stop and consider that God is a "fiercely jealous lover"? For me? For you? Someone is fiercely jealous for us?

In his love, his wholly unconditional love, God fiercely loves you and me with a jealous love. He is not content for us just to want some of his love. No, he wants us to want all of his love, and he is fiercely jealous, yes envious, of any love that competes with his. God is God, and he wants no rivals. No idols.

This is the beautiful side of envy. Envy that is motivated by a Lover with the purest of intentions. God wants us to have a love that does not envy in our hearts. And it is only knowing this kind of love from God that can reduce the influence and inflow of envy into our hearts and lives. When we rest in God's love, contentment and gratefulness are the fruit of seeing what is already ours. Then and only then will we see what truly matters most. Then and only then will the path before us become clear as his love changes the priorities in our hearts. Then and only then will we keep traveling the road of God's unconditional love, his most excellent way. Then and only then, I'll be content to boast about the ice cubes in my fridge instead of coveting the ice cubes hanging from someone's ears.

Speaking of boasting . . .

Content-ment and gratefulness are the greatest antidotes to the poison of envy that jaundices our souls. You see, here in the valley, you and I were never meant to arrive.

CHAPTER NINE

Make Love, Not Wal-Mart

Boasting provides a peek into the soul of another person only to reveal an aching hollowness yearning to be filled with praise, acceptance, and belonging.

You know you've been married for a long time when you're right in the middle of making passionate love with your wife and she says, "Hey, have you seen that new Wal-Mart?"

Happened to a friend of mine.

The way he tells the story, oh my goodness, talk about performance anxiety.

Interruptus maximus.

His sex life has never been the same since the day Wal-Mart moved into town.

Now normally, my friend's a confident kinda guy. He has a healthy, fun-loving relationship with his wife, but I really feel for him. Between sex and sales, it's almost impossible to compete with a superstore. My friend, there's only one of him. Wal-Mart? The place has seared their established retail brand identity on the minds of women worldwide. Wherever my buddy's wife goes, Wal-Mart is there.

Like me, my buddy has four children. He's a regular Virile Merrill and his wife's a Fertile Myrtle, so I found it a bit surprising to hear that a superstore had come between them. When the two of them are in bed, my buddy's as focused as a Navy fighter pilot performing an aircraft carrier night landing on stormy seas, but his wife gets swept away in a Wal-Mart Aisle 7 fantasy, enraptured in the ecstasy of sorting through rack after rack of deep-discounted children's clothes.

Oh, forget it. I give up.

I can't carry on this ruse any longer.

There is no friend. No buddy.

Wal-Mart. It happened to me.

Okay, four kids later, maybe I've become a bit overconfident in establishing my own name brand identity. Instead of bending a humble knee and offering a prayer of thanksgiving for lovemaking afterglow, I'll admit that I go totally Hollywood. I disco dance on the nightstand. I spike my pillow like a pigskin football. Moonwalk over the duvet. High-five the reading lamp. Occasionally, I'll even tear outside and run around the neighborhood with fists raised, screaming, "YESSS," while the neighborhood dogs howl my name and their owners call me other sorts of names.

Then I fall asleep.

So as you can see, it's extremely embarrassing to be humbled by my wife's Wal-Mart fantasy life. I'm a lover, not a shopper. For all I know, she may be physically present as we unwrap our exquisite Happy Meals by candlelight, but in her mind, she's miles from me as she envisions herself in K-Mart, racing down Aisle 4 for a Blue Light Special and filling her shopping basket with drastically reduced baby wipes and Juicy-Juice.

What guy with flowers and candlelight can compete with a storewide supersale that lasts for days?

And I thought I really knew her.

So what's Krista's latest fantasy?

A Memorial Day sale at Michael's? A Back-to-School sale at Old Navy?

The first few years of our marriage, Krista didn't call me Mr. Stud Muffin for my baking exploits. But after having four little buns in the oven, my raw physical prowess doesn't seem to impress her like it used to. I now see that our love life is a tricky proposition. Ladies, you know what I'm talking about. For couples who've been married a few years, lovemaking can last as long as a quarter-horse race or three entire commercials between your favorite shows. Considering a woman's mood, the lunar rotation, what time of night it is, if the trash has been taken out or not, or whether a girlfriend is mad at her for some reason she can't figure out, us guys never really know if tonight's the night for love. If it's not a school night . . . or if she feels really charged about how supportive and caring you were about all the money she saved you on the sales she scored earlier that day at Wal-Mart, who knows what us guys are in for?

Despite the utter unpredictability of it all, I have discovered a little secret that will light the passion of the most indifferent women. Yes, men, this will get your wife all hot and bothered.

Half-annual sale at Nordstrom.

Let your wife go wild at Nordstrom and believe me, you'll thank me later.

I know I can't put all of this on my wife and Wal-Mart. I'm just like any other guy—I measure my manhood by my performance. I do, therefore I am. I'm a conqueror. If another suitor like Wal-Mart wanders into the picture, I get competitive. I couldn't care less about their sales and deep discounts. But maybe, just maybe, I've become too overconfident. A little too proud. Too boastful.

I must confess that my boasting isn't limited to my bedroom gymnastics. Ask Krista and she'll confirm that I boast and brag all over our home, drawing attention to myself for the simplest of chores. I don't do this all the time, because there are only so many ways I can impress my wife with doing the dishes. But when it comes to home improvements, I can get pretty cocky about what other guys pay to get done.

My boasting provides my wife a chance to celebrate my home improvement successes, pulling her out of a deep existential despair and providing her a profound sense of ultimate meaning and purpose. Nothing makes her day more than when I point out with great pride, "Look, dear, I fixed the water stopper in the bathtub. Look at how well mowed that lawn is. Look at how I organized the junk drawer. Look at that rose garden I just planted. Look at how clean your car is." Like I said, I'm wired for performance. I like my home improvements to be recognized for their artistic merit.

Though I may joke about my boasting, it is a deep spiritual problem because it exalts a part of us that has never known what it is like to be accepted. Boasting reveals an identity tied to accomplishments, possessions, position, or financial status. Or even spiritual pride. Boasting is an individual spiritual identity problem, but when both husband and wife tie their identities to where they live and what they do and how much they own and who they know, boasting becomes a shared sin of covering up what we want to remain hidden. Boasting exalts an insecure self and strips the marriage relationship from a deeper, more satisfying bond of resting in God's unconditional love.

Marriage is a perfect opportunity to burst one another's bubble. Pride loves to hide in silence, and instead of pulling our spouses' feet back down to the ground when their heads begin to swell with the gases of self-absorption, we stay silent instead of pulling out a long and very sharp pin. Proverbs 27:17 says, "As iron sharpens iron, so one man sharpens another." Spiritual

Boasting reveals an identity tied to accomplishments, possessions, position, or financial status. Or even spiritual pride.

and marital intimacy cannot be separated from character development, which is why a husband and wife can help one another grow by sharpening one another with an occasional reality check. Urging the people of Rome to keep from exalting themselves over one another, Paul wrote, "For by the grace given me I say to every one of you: Do not think of yourself more highly than you ought, but rather think of yourself with sober judgment, in accordance with the measure of faith God has given you" (Rom. 12:3). As individuals and couples, we are to walk in grace and in faith. Not with swollen heads, hidden pride, or gaseous boasting.

Living in South Orange County, I see a lot of success. Lots of diamonds like ice cubes. The place is dripping with moola, even though the poor are among us. I have met very successful, humble couples who recognize everything they have comes from God and who love to be silent, quiet givers of their wealth. I've also met more than a few couples who, to put it bluntly, are boastful people. They are the type of couples Stanley Thomas wrote about in his book *The Millionaire Next Door*. Couples who appear to own a lot on the outside but who have no real net worth. Thomas writes that these kinds of people live in opulent homes, drive exotic cars, go on tropical vacations, and have nannies for the nanny who parents the kids. These folks are leveraged to the hilt, and when you talk to them, you sense a deep spiritual hunger in their lives. They are quick to mention the newest car they bought. The latest vacation. How much was spent on the last shopping spree. All to fill the vacuum in their hearts that was meant to hold the heart of God. And these people are in our churches. They're not much different from me or you, because boasting isn't limited to what we have or own. It's anything that bloats us up bigger than we really are.

I recently sat in a meeting with a brilliant man of faith who had an obvious low view of himself. Or maybe too high a view of himself, I'm not sure. Within the first few minutes of our conversation, I was more than a bit surprised at how quick he was to drop the names of all his important, well-known personal friends. During our time together at lunch, he told me about a personal meeting with such and such a high-ranking pastor. And then there was his phone conversation with this well-known Christian leader. And this lunch appointment with a famous business leader. From time to time, he lowered his voice in feigned humility, but then he'd rattle off a new name or two. I was impressed he could remember his calendar that far back, but his name-dropping was nauseating. And actually quite sad.

I'm sure Paul knew a lot of famous people. He preached the gospel before kings, rulers, and all the important religious leaders of his day, which could have given him plenty of opportunity to name-drop. His fifteen minutes of fame could have lasted for weeks. But was Paul impressed with all the famous people he knew? No, Paul was impressed with one person and one person only. "May I never boast except in the cross of our Lord Jesus Christ, through which the world has been crucified to me, and I to the world" (Gal. 6:14).

Paul's heart was riveted to the heart of God. He chose to boast about God instead of himself. His one and only boast was the cross of Jesus Christ. What could Paul boast about that could ever be greater than the love of God? When you and I boast about ourselves, what we own, or the hordes of famous people we know, we lower our view of who God says we are as his children and, ultimately, lower our view of God.

We boast to bring attention to ourselves instead of glory to God. We want to make a name for ourselves instead of being named by God. We want to see our name in lights to hide the darkness of our need. We clamor for attention to prove we are worthy of someone's love. We boast and brag to one another, but we boast and brag to the wrong person. The ones to whom we boast are not capable of giving us what we need. What we need is unconditional love. The unconditional love that comes from God, who loves us in spite of our shame.

But when we speak of our blessings in a humble, grateful manner instead of boasting, we direct everyone's attention to God. Instead of living as if the universe revolves around us, we recognize that God is the source of all life and all our blessings. Instead of boasting, we're amazed that he would allow us to receive such gracious gifts. William Barclay wrote, "The real lover cannot get over the wonder that it is loved. Love is kept humble by the consciousness that it can never offer its loved one a gift which is good enough."[2]

If our core source material for conversation and connecting with others is nothing more than talking about ourselves, we are only revealing our deep desire to be loved, which may offer us hope if we can somehow become aware of this deep need. In expressing his concern for the Corinthians, Paul said, "If I must boast, I will boast of the things that show my weakness." If we're going to boast, let's at least boast about the love we need.

How much of our boasting springs from our childhood? How many of us spent our early years feeling like the Invisible Man? I can remember many Saturday afternoons watching the Invisible Man unwrap himself into nothingness. Wrapped in outer clothes and bandages around the face, the Invisible Man could be seen and talked to, but nobody really knew who he was. Nobody could see the real person, only the shell of what he wore on the outside. Once all the outer garments were taken away, all that was left was an invisible, unseen Self.

Do we live in an individualistic, narcissistic nation because of a deep, collective fear of not being seen? It's ironic that in our desire to exalt our individuality, we isolate ourselves from each other and the deep need we have to be known and belong. By boasting, we give the pretense that we've arrived. That we really do have our act together. But we all know that's a lie, because nobody in the valley has their act together. We are all messes in progress.

> How much of our boasting springs from our childhood? How many of us spent our early years feeling like the Invisible Man?

Our boasting offers a distorted view of who we really are, much like the view we get when we walk through a Hall of Mirrors at a carnival. Our strengths are magnified and our weaknesses minimized. We offer a false picture to the people in our lives who have yet to discover who we really are. By pretending, we isolate ourselves from the Christian community God designed to bring us hope and healing.

Sometimes it takes a monk to tell us how it is. Thomas Merton wrote:

> It is therefore of supreme importance that we consent to live not for ourselves but for others. When we do this we will be able first of all to face and accept our own limitations. As long as we secretly adore ourselves, our own deficiencies will remain to torture us with an apparent defilement. But if we live for others, we will gradually discover that no one expects us to be "as gods." We will see that we are human, like everyone else, that we all have weaknesses and deficiencies, and that these limitations of ours play a most important part in all our lives. It is because we need others and others need us. We are not all weak in the same spots, and so we supplement and complete one another, each one making up in himself for the lack of another.[3]

If I know who I am as a beloved child of God, I don't have to boast. I don't have to brag. I already have a heavenly Father boasting on my behalf. What achievement, what accomplishment, what pinnacle of success can I reach that will ever compare with the lavish love God offers me every moment of the day? What job promotion, new purchase, or possession will ever be able to measure up against the free gift of God's unconditional love?

> If I know who I am as a beloved child of God, I don't have to boast. I don't have to brag. I already have a heavenly Father boasting on my behalf.

If we know that we are dearly loved as God's children, isn't that enough? It is enough. God's love is enough for you and me. Secure in our identity as his children, as people who belong, we don't have to preen and primp, strut and position ourselves to be recognized. We don't need to draw attention to ourselves, because we already have the full attention of our Father. We are seen and loved as we are. At this very moment. Why boast when you already belong?

Jeremiah wrote,

> This is what the LORD says:
> "Let not the wise man boast of his wisdom
>   or the strong man boast of his strength
>   or the rich man boast of his riches,
> but let him who boasts boast about this:
>   that he understands and knows me,
> that I am the LORD who exercises kindness,
>   justice and righteousness on the earth,
>   for in these I delight."
>
> *Jeremiah 9:23–24*

You can boast in your own wisdom. You can boast about your biceps or low body fat. You can boast in your riches. Or you can boast about this: You know God. And because you personally know God, you delight in kindness, justice, and righteousness. There's nothing wrong with exercise, but Paul said to make sure you know where your priorities are. "Train yourself to be godly. For physical training is of some value, but godliness has value for all things, holding promise for both the present life and the life to come" (1 Tim. 4:7–8).

Go to the gym. Get strong as you train your heart to love like God loves. If God's given you a mind, knock yourself out and use your intellect like Einstein as you pursue the God of all wisdom. If you're rolling in the dough, let it roll out of your pocket as you give to others what God has so graciously given to you. People talk about what they love. Delighting in what God delights in is evidence of the condition of your heart.

If Jeremiah were peering over your shoulder right now as you read, he might whisper these words: Do you delight in what the Lord delights in? As a couple, do you delight in kindness, justice, and righteousness? Or does your boasting rub off on your spouse? Are you partners in pretension? Are you moving each other toward humility, or do you as a couple boast in one another's stuff and successes? Do you build up and affirm your spouse by talking about their character? Do you boast about your spouse (in a positive sense) by showing true appreciation for who they are instead of what they earn or do? Is it clear to those around you who and what you really delight in?

Love does not boast, because love is not concerned with itself. Love lives to give itself away, and it's far too modest to boast about it. When you stop and think about it, you and I don't have time to boast. Life is far too short for blowing our own horn. It could be over in a breath. Or our last boast. Maybe the cure for boasting is to stop looking at life from our limited perspective and expand our view of who's really in charge of this spinning orb we live on.

Now listen, you who say, "Today or tomorrow we will go to this or that city, spend a year there, carry on business and make money." Why, you do not even know what will happen tomorrow. What is your life? You are a mist that appears for a little while and then vanishes. Instead, you ought to say, "If it is the Lord's will, we will live and do this or that." As it is, you boast and brag. All such boasting is evil.

James 4:13–16

I'm going to have Krista read that verse. Maybe that will stop her Wal-Mart monkey business and shopping shenanigans.

Or maybe I'll just open up shop down the street. If I start small, work hard, and offer the deepest discounts Wal-Mart has ever seen, minivan moms will flock to my store for wipes and Juicy-Juice. Then I'll open gigantic stores in all fifty states, go public on Wall Street, become the next big store billionaire, and win my wife back. If it's the Lord's will, that is.

But if I win over Wal-Mart, will I win at love? Or will I just become proud?

CHAPTER TEN

Proud Mary

Pride prevents love from flowing in relationships in that it chooses to dig foxholes instead of mending fences. It is the ultimate downfall of men and women who prefer to be right rather than forgiven.

My plane touched down in Denver. I'd been asked to speak at a conference for an international women's ministry dedicated to serving exhausted mothers of preschoolers, also known as MOPS. Krista had been involved in MOPS for years, and I am a big fan of their dedication to moms and kids. We've had little toddlers running throughout our home the past twelve years, so any person or organization that can pull my wife back from the brink of insanity after a long day of spills, thrills, and chills has got to be a good thing.

After disembarking, I was met at the gate by a man in his midforties who'd volunteered to drive the incoming conference speakers to the hotel. There were one or two other estrogen-challenged presenters who'd be speaking at the conference, so I knew I wouldn't be alone, but I was already feeling more than a bit self-conscious. I was still at the airport, about forty minutes from my hotel, and already I could feel the waves of estrogen advancing on the Denver area like a major winter storm system.

Great, I thought to myself. What have I gotten myself into?

Four thousand women from all over the United States had just left home for the weekend. Rejoicing. In my mind, I clearly saw the other half of this equation: Husbands from Hawaii all the way to the tip of Maine left standing on the front porch with 3.2 children, waving good-bye, appearing as if bathing, dressing, feeding, and caring for their offspring, alone, was just another day at the office. Children or no children, every woman knows that beneath this thin male façade of confidence is the feeling of stark raving terror. The kids will not eat a balanced diet of grains, leafy greens, cage-free chicken protein, and organic colon-cleansing corn husks. No, while all the moms are whooping it up in Denver, the dads will poison their children with Pez candy, Captain Crunch cereal, 7-Eleven Slurpees, and Happy Meals from Mickey D's. The kids will not go to bed on time. They will fall asleep in the living room in a media-induced coma after the eleventh Blockbuster video of the day, and they will wake up on the couch late Sunday morning when Dad rushes them into the car half-dressed, mismatched, and uncombed, only to arrive at church forty-five minutes late with all the other dads who are doing exactly the same thing, if they even make it at all.

My driver introduced himself as Tim and shook my hand. We proceeded to the baggage area, making small talk about airplane travel. Tim mentioned his wife was along with him on this trip to the airport. She was meeting another woman, a well-known women's ministry conference speaker, at a different gate. I'd never heard of her, but that didn't mean much because she'd probably never heard of me either. I knew I wasn't well known. Except, of course, to my wife and kids, the IRS, and the boy whose bike spokes I rammed with a broom pole back in sixth grade.

Anyway, the four of us soon met up, exchanged pleasantries, and proceeded to Tim's minivan. Tim and I sat in front; the women sat behind us in the passenger seats. Tim navigated his way out of the airport as a polite conversation ensued, mainly focused on where the two of us were from. Whether we had children or not. What our hometowns were like. The general, friendly sorts of questions that complete strangers ask rather than endure forty minutes of traffic in silence. The couple from Colorado were genuinely nice. Friendly. Glad to be of service. Not put out by meeting strangers at the airport on their day off.

The well-known conference speaker was petite and attractive. At first glance, it seemed the years had been kind to her. But by the sound of her voice, she did seem a bit high-strung. A little too intense. Perhaps my presumption was incorrect. Maybe it was a wrong first impression or maybe it was her hair that was pulled back as taut as Glad-wrap over a tuna casserole that made her appear so uptight. Though I usually try to give people the benefit of the doubt, I couldn't shake the feeling that she carried about an air of self-importance.

I was from California, the land of fruits and nuts, which already made me suspect. She was from Oklahoma, a state name that, as a kid, always reminded me of oatmeal. But oatmeal's good. I like oatmeal.

As Tim pulled onto the freeway, our polite conversation took a wrong turn in an amazing flip of linguistic gymnastics. The woman from Oklahoma asked me what topic I was speaking on at the conference. I told her politely that I worked with grieving families and was going to speak about how to talk to children about funerals, death, and grief, and how to answer the many fun and insightful questions kids ask about heaven. This is a seminar I generally have to pay people to attend, because there's an unspoken belief that if you attend a seminar like mine, within forty-eight hours someone in your immediate family will get run over by a trolley car or get electrocuted while changing a lightbulb in an Elmo lamp. I don't know what it is, but people are not into death.

I almost laughed when I told her my speaking topic, because the universal response is almost always something in the vein of, "Oh, how interesting . . ." Now that the woman realized she was driving with the Angel of Death, I was almost positive she made furtive glances at the door locks all the way into downtown.

To ease the morbid look on her face, I told her, as I tell everyone in awkward situations like this, that my family's been in the funeral business for over a hundred years and that death runs in our family. Ha ha. Get it? My dad's the last one to let you down! *Pah-dump-pah!* Yeah, and we just had lady fingers for dinner last night.

Okay, I'll stop now.

She was not amused, so I asked her what she was speaking about.

"Oh," she said, perking up. "I'm speaking about prayer."

Death and prayer. There seems to be a pretty close relationship between the two.

"That's great," I replied. "Prayer's a good thing."

Tim and his wife nodded in agreement.

The woman smiled and asked me another question. "Have you written a book about death or children or grief?"

I said yes and told her the title. She came right back and said in an excited, well-don't-you-know tone of voice, "I've written two best-selling books on prayer. I travel all over the country speaking to women and churches and conferences on the importance of prayer."

"That's great," I replied, acknowledging her achievements and notoriety. Then, in a staccato-burst of questions, she fired at me like a hand-cranked Gatling gun.

"Do you speak very often? Do you travel much? Do you do a lot of conferences?"

"No. Not that much," I responded, none too sheepishly. In fact, I don't speak a lot. I don't travel a lot. I don't do a lot of conferences. My favorite place is sitting at the dinner table with Krista and the kids. Besides, most death books don't sell millions of copies. Parents do not rush into stores to buy books for their kids explaining terminal illness and caskets and cremation, any more than they rush into mortuaries to do prearrangement funeral planning for themselves.

As I was trapped in Tim's minivan, the tide of the conversation turned against me in the form of an interrogation.

"Oh, Joey," Annie Oakley said, taking aim again. (Names have been changed to protect the not-so-innocent.) "Did you attend the groundbreaking ceremonies of such and such ministry center?" she piped, mentioning the opening of a large family ministry based in Colorado Springs.

"No, I didn't attend," I politely replied again. By now, I was way past wrong first impressions. And because Tim and I had just met, there was no way for me to signal him to rescue me. No code word or third-base-coach hand signals.

"Oh, my husband and I are good friends of so and so, and I've been on his radio show a number of times. Have you ever been on so and so's radio show?"

"No, I've never been on his show," I said, as if it didn't really matter. Then I said a silent prayer, asking God to help me exercise extreme amounts of self-control.

"Well, my literary agent is also in Colorado. He's just done such a marvelous job for me," she prattled on. "Do you have a literary agent, Joey?"

No, lady, I was thinking to myself. I don't have an agent. I'm going to take the 15 percent my agent would have received from my book sales and have my eardrums surgically removed.

Had you been in the car, you would have sworn by the stench permeating the air that this lady's lifework wasn't dedicated to helping moms learn how to pray for the safety of their children left home with dad for the weekend. Like me, you would have done a double take and sworn on your firstborn that this woman was a bona fide, tobacco-spitting, Oklahoman steer rancher. The air in our covered wagon was so full of her self-absorbed prattling about my-ministry this and my-best-selling-book that that our car could have run out of gas and stayed at a steady sixty miles an hour.

After a while, Annie Oakley lost interest in my mere mortal status, and the conversation seemed to dribble underneath the floor mat. Slowly I turned toward Tim, who was staring straight ahead at the traffic, content to be in the driver's seat instead of being the hapless sap riding shotgun and taking all the bullets.

I asked Tim what kind of work he did, which is the safest, most mundane question known to humankind. But right then I needed safe. Of course, if Tim were to say that he'd just locked up his speaking schedule for the next two years, I knew I would jump into oncoming traffic. But Tim didn't say that. Quietly, in an awkward tone of voice, Tim said that he worked on the staff of a large men's ministry but was soon to lose his job. The organization was having financial troubles, and a large number of men were getting laid off.

When Tim told me he was losing his job, he said it almost matter-of-factly. His honesty reminded me of when I lost my job a few years earlier. Not knowing what to do with the grief and fear pushed down deep in my heart, I told people about it in the same way. Due to budget restraints and scarcity of resources, the situation was a reality beyond my control. But inside, I was scared spitless.

Tim and I chatted about his job loss and family and kids and Denver trivia, and before I knew it, we were at our hotel near the convention center. I thanked Tim and his wife for picking us up and driving us to the hotel. Then Annie and I shared sincere good-byes as we each headed our separate ways.

As I entered my empty hotel room, I thought about my drive from the airport. What a study in contrasts. Here was a guy losing his job who's spending his Saturday driving around me and a woman who can't stop talking about the importance of her nationwide prayer job and her Mini-Me ministry. Like he wouldn't rather be sitting in his La-Z-Boy and watching a Bronco's game.

Later, I called Krista to see how she and the kids were doing. I told her about my little airport adventure and gave her my permission to shoot me on sight if I ever talked like that, acted like that, or attempted to make myself one inch taller than my five-foot-ten frame.

Come to think of it, maybe that wasn't such a good idea. What if Krista takes me up on it and applies for a hunting license? Because as much as Annie Oakley chafed me raw, I have to admit that if the success fairies had showered their golden pixie dust on me, would I be taking a vow of poverty, humility, and a life of cloistered prayer? Didn't I want the masses to buy my books, invite me to symposiums in Switzerland, and create traffic problems at Barnes and Noble book signings? Didn't I want to appear on every major network television station and tell my publicist that my schedule was so jam-packed that Oprah would have to take a number? Nah . . . not me.

Sorry, I know myself better than that. Annie Oakley and I have a lot in common, more than I was willing to admit at the time. I'm subject to my own delusions of grandeur just like any writer who sits at a keyboard piecing together words one letter at a time. Annie may have worn her pride on the outside, but more often than not, I wear it on the inside, where it likes to hide in false humility. Maybe what bugged me about her is the same thing that bugs me about myself.

Pride is the hidden sin, the quiet idol to oneself that loves to reside in the corners of our hearts. But in outward displays, we can flaunt pride in our marriages with stubbornness, inflexibility, obstinacy, and refusal to show weakness. Pride prevents love from flowing in relationships in that it chooses to dig foxholes instead of mending fences. It is the ultimate downfall of men and women who prefer to be right rather than forgiven. Shakespeare wrote, "He that is proud eats himself up." That is the nature of pride.

> Pride is the hidden sin, the quiet idol to oneself that loves to reside in the corners of our hearts.

Pride wedges itself in between relationships, separating husbands and wives from the intimacy and the desire for oneness that drew them together in the first place. Pride isolates us from relationship and keeps us from saying sorry when we know we're wrong. Pride needs a crowbar to open our lips with the two most difficult words known to humankind: I'm sorry. Instead of counting our losses and moving to forgiveness, because of our pride, we let things escalate. Instead of working through conflict and winning for one another and the marriage, we man our battle stations waiting for the other person to wave the white flag. How often do we fight just to win? Just to be right? Just to prove we can dish it out? And at what cost?

What we learn from Paul is that love is not proud. In layman's terms, love does not have a big head. It doesn't try to make itself out to be any greater than it is. Love does not have an exalted opinion of itself but always seeks to exalt the loveliness of the Beloved. Healthy pride, like being proud of your wife and kids or a job well done, confers dignity and respect, but this is always out of a position of humility and not arrogance. Love doesn't seek to intimidate or posture with an abuse of power. Power and position, the means for control and domination in corporate settings, get old real quick on the home front.

Are you prideful? Does your pride get in the way of love? Does your marriage get stuck because of your tendency to dig in your heels? Does your pride mask itself by being overly sensitive or digging up the past as old ammo for the present conflict? Do you really believe, like some do, that love means you never have to say you're sorry? Does your pride vaunt itself by thinking that if your spouse really demonstrates unconditional love toward you, then you don't have to change? You may not think like this, but there are far too many people who do.

> Healthy pride, like being proud of your wife and kids or a job well done, confers dignity and respect, but this is always out of a position of humility and not arrogance.

Or does your love for God lead you on the path of humility? Do you have a hunger for humility, realizing the depth of God's humility shown toward you by loving you at all costs? Even at the cost of his Son's life? Philippians 2:8 tells us that Jesus "humbled himself and became obedient to death—even death on a cross!" Humility always requires the death of pride, and our pride wants anything but a slow death.

As you can imagine, God has more than a few opinions about pride.

"I hate pride and arrogance, evil behavior and perverse speech" (Prov. 8:13). God doesn't mess around with what he loves and what he hates.

"The LORD detests all the proud of heart. Be sure of this: They will not go unpunished" (Prov. 16:5). Here we see a distinct correlation between pride and punishment. The choice is ours.

"In his pride the wicked does not seek him; in all his thoughts there is no room for God" (Ps. 10:4). Pride pushes out any thought of seeking a higher authority. Pride makes itself its own authority, which ultimately leads to its own downfall.

"Before his downfall a man's heart is proud, but humility comes before honor" (Prov. 18:12). Pride before a fall is not a new idea, but how often do we seek God and the honor he bestows on those who seek him instead of trusting in our own self-sufficiency? When Paul lived and worked among the Corinthian people, he was surrounded by a whole city of Greeks, Romans, and Jews with plenty of reasons to pride themselves on their self-sufficiency. The Corinthians were the cosmopolitan sophisticates of their day. They lived with a carpe diem, party-hard attitude. The word itself, *Corinth,* means satisfied and beautiful. When you're wealthy, who needs God? Who needs salvation if all your needs are met?

The Corinthians clothed themselves in pride, much like we do ourselves. We think we don't need God's unconditional love, but we do. When we're in conflict with our spouses, we feel like we don't need their love, but we do. It's pride that makes us unwilling to look at a problem or conflict from our spouses' perspectives. Pride makes us stubborn as mules and unyielding as a goat chewing on an old shoe. I know it's not politically correct to stereotype animals, but scientists don't call a bunch of lions a "pride of lions" for no good reason. Go up against a pride of lions and see what I mean.

In the love story of Hosea, God likens himself to a lion, as well as a few other ferocious beasts. He has a word or two to share with the nation of Israel about its pride.

> But I am the LORD your God,
>   who brought you out of Egypt.
> You shall acknowledge no God but me,
>   no Savior except me.
> I cared for you in the desert,
>   in the land of burning heat.
> When I fed them, they were satisfied;

when they were satisfied, they became proud;
  then they forgot me.
So I will come upon them like a lion,
  like a leopard I will lurk by the path.
Like a bear robbed of her cubs,
  I will attack them and rip them open.
Like a lion I will devour them;
  a wild animal will tear them apart.

Hosea 13:4–8

God's passion for his people is no kid's story a la *The Wizard of Oz:* "Lions and tigers and bears . . . oh my!" God is serious about our pride. To the nation of Israel, God says his unconditional love is so strong, so powerful, and so ferocious that he is willing to devour Israel to get her attention. In Christ, we have received mercy and grace and freedom, but our response is to be one of gratefulness and humility, because when we are pride-filled, we set ourselves in direct opposition to God. When it comes to pride, God is *muy serioso.* Decisive humility is a choice that can change the prideful condition of our hearts to pursue the better conditions of God's unconditional love. Humility will always bring us closer to God and one another.

I came to that convention with seventy-five books to sell and left with sixty-six. You do the math. It was an exercise in humility. I bet Annie sold a wagon train full of books. Maybe God was trying to teach me something.

As I stood in front of the hotel waiting for my ride to the

> Decisive humility is a choice that can change the prideful condition of our hearts to pursue the better conditions of God's unconditional love. Humility will always bring us closer to God and one another.

139

airport when the convention was over, little did I know that God was bringing me a new travel companion to show me a better way than the way of my pride. A more excellent way consistent with the kind of man and husband and father God wants me to be.

A van pulled up to the curb. A different driver this time. No Tim inside. I hopped in and joined a woman heading home from the convention like me.

Her name was Mary.

Mary was a regional director of MOPS, a volunteer position giving leadership and mentoring to local MOPS groups. I don't remember where Mary was from, somewhere in the Midwest. She told me she'd received an urgent phone call the night before from her husband informing her that her twelve-year-old daughter was very sick and had been rushed to the hospital. Her daughter was so sick, intensive-care sick, that she might die in the hospital before Mary arrived home. Not the type of phone call you want to get when you're a thousand miles away from home and can't get a flight out until the next morning.

The previous Thursday, the day Mary left for the convention, her daughter said she felt like she was coming down with something. On Friday, she spent most of the day in bed. By the time Saturday rolled around, Mary's husband watched his daughter's condition worsen. Off to the hospital for a quick series of tests, and the doctors soon discovered that a rare virus was attacking the young girl's body. The doctors informed Mary's husband that the virus was spreading rapidly. Potentially lethal. As Mary relayed the urgency of her crisis to me, a complete stranger, I was amazed at her composure and sense of calm. Scared, yes. Concerned, you bet, but not freaking out like I would be.

"I tried to get a flight back home last night but wasn't able to," she said in a soft, hushed voice. "But I have prayed about this. God knows how I wanted to get home as soon as possible, but the Lord has given me peace. Her life is in his hands."

I listened to Mary's story with a quiet awe and utter inability to be of much help, except to listen as she recounted the details of the past day. Her daughter could very well die from this virus, yet Mary had a laserlike peace. The same kind of incredible peace that Paul said surpasses all human understanding. Her peace wasn't a cold detachment or an "oh well" determinism. Mary had the right perspective on pride. She wasn't proud. She was engaged in the crisis but not overwhelmed by it. Without a doubt, she was rattled by the severity of her daughter's illness, but she was rallying against her fears through prayer.

Pride usually doesn't rear its head when a parent is asking God to save the life of a son or daughter. Desperation has a peculiar way of humbling us. Maybe Mary had lingered over these words and found just what she needed: "God opposes the proud but gives grace to the humble" (James 4:6).

Two rides. Two people of prayer. A little pride sandwiched in between.

I am more like the former than the latter, but there's no telling what can happen if I choose the way of love. The same is true for you. And it all begins with the grace that comes from God in humble prayer.

Love is not proud.

Mary had chosen a better way, and it would not be taken from her. Is there any more excellent way to travel through the valley than this?

From humility comes the sweet smell of love.

CHAPTER ELEVEN

The Sweet Smell of Love

We know the smell of love exactly for what it is. Love offers beauty and goodness. It permeates the air around us with an unmistakable and attractive fragrance. True unconditional love makes sweet-smelling deposits in the heart of the beloved.

Every spring, Krista looks forward to the emergence of her favorite wildflower, sweet peas. After winter has dropped enough rain to make all of us Southern Californians mildly uncomfortable, the sweet peas pop up with the familiarity of a lifelong friend visiting from out of town. Dotting the hillside in nearby Capistrano Beach with pink, red, and lavender blossoms, the sweet peas and their intoxicating fragrance make the collection of the sticky green stems worth the effort. Their budding creates an anticipation and excitement, a blooming in my wife you could say, that is not easily replicated.

For the past couple weeks Krista had been dropping hints here and there about this year's bloom and how I'd better move quickly before it was all over. So one Sunday after swimming with the kids at a local pool, I drove through Capistrano Beach to the hillside where we do our annual sweet pea picking. Janae and I hopped out while the boys stayed in the car. I was wearing my flip-flops, not exactly the best climbing shoes for a steep slope.

Smelling and oohing and aahing, Janae and I picked and picked. The milky sap felt like Elmer's glue on our fingers as we lovingly gathered one sweet pea after another. Tottering back and forth on the steep hillside, we laughed as we each almost lost our balance and tumbled down the hill. "Mom's going to love these sweet peas," we said to one another as we picked as quickly as possible. For the short wildflower season, delivering a small, itty-bitty bunch of sweet peas is minor league. In no way does it deliver the emotional home-run blast of a big bunch bursting with color.

After Janae gathered her bunch and I had mine, we started down the hill to the car. I had taken only three steps down the slippery slope when wham! My feet went out from under me, and I came down on a patch of dirt in such a forceful way, I experienced what a pilot friend of mine would call a "hard landing." A bum deal would be an understatement. Janae laughed as I picked my sore patootie off the ground. We slipped and skittered our way back to the car as I moaned about my aching rear.

When we pulled up into the driveway, Krista walked into the garage from the back door. When she peered through the front windshield and saw Janae holding the biggest bunch of sweet peas we'd ever picked, a huge smile lit up across her face.

"Deposits! Deposits! Deposits!" she cried.

Janae and I smacked this one out of the park.

Krista grabbed the sweet peas and inhaled deeply. "Oh, they smell so good!"

143

Isn't that the way of love? Love always smells so sweet. It permeates the air around us with an unmistakable and attractive fragrance. True unconditional love makes sweet-smelling deposits in the heart of the beloved. That is exactly what Krista was referring to when she shouted "Deposits!" Now, I don't always get love right. I don't bring home flowers every day, especially sweet peas that only bloom once a year. But choosing the way of unconditional love is not a complicated scientific equation or a matter of fate left to the shifting whims of our feelings. God never would have offered to show us the way of unconditional love if he hadn't intended to give us the strength and courage to walk it.

Marriage is a matter of choosing to make more deposits than withdrawals in the heart of our beloved. And remember, love doesn't have to depend on your own will or strength. Every good and perfect gift comes from God (James 1:17), and the power to bring the sweet smell of unconditional love into your marriage comes from him.

Not far from the hillside where Janae and I picked the sweet peas is the Doheny Beach sanitation plant (DBSP). You do not want to go near the sanitation plant on methane day. You'd swear you were at a burrito convention. In the nearby neighborhoods, realtors take prospective buyers into listed homes only on certain days of the month. Who wants to live in a home filled with foul air? If I were to bottle conditional love, I know the perfect source. One whiff of DBSP and you'll be heading for the hills.

No doubt Paul had more than a few whiffs of conditional love before he wrote, "Love is not rude." Through the Holy Spirit, Paul gave us the choice of a more excellent way. Every day in our marriages, we have the choice to make sweet-pea deposits or rude withdrawals. Do we live in such a way that our words and actions are as pleasurable as picking sweet peas on a hillside? Do our lives add color and fragrance to those around us? When we enter a room, do our spouses and kids come to embrace us or do they run to avoid the foul scent we're giving off?

Sweet-pea deposits of love, courtesy, and consideration are the fragrant wildflowers that can cover the rolling hillsides as we travel together through life in the valley. They make the journey so much more enjoyable than passing by the stark, industrial coldness of a sanitation plant. But there are days when you and I make the choice to pull into the Doheny Beach sanitation plant, don't we? Though we know a stinging comment or a selfish act stinks, we do it anyway. We rationalize that we're just letting off steam because we're angry or frustrated. But let's call our rudeness for what it is: bad gas.

The problem with rudeness is that stinking rude is remembered. The smell of rude withdrawals lingers much longer than the fading bloom of sweet-pea deposits. Did you know that the word *rude* appears only once in the Bible? Did God use this word once because it smells so bad? Think of all the adjectives associated with a rude, crude, and socially unacceptable person. A rude individual is impolite, discourteous, bad-mannered, uncouth, coarse, foulmouthed, offensive, insulting, nasty, odious, boorish. I love those last two words.

Next time your spouse is rude to you, assume a heavy British accent and proclaim, "Enough! You are being odious and boorish!"

Your new vocabulary can be an effective tool for knocking the rude offender off guard. Rude is offensive because it immediately puts people on the defensive. When you smell something rude, isn't your immediate reaction to back away? Find sanctuary from the

> Sweet-pea deposits of love, courtesy, and consideration are the fragrant wildflowers that can cover the rolling hillsides as we travel together through life in the valley.

smell? Though running from the smell of rudeness is instinctive, we are also wired to react. When we are *sprayed* by an unkind word or deed from our spouse, our immediate reaction is to repel the rude offender with a little rudeness of our own. We want to *spray back*. The only problem with spraying one another back and forth is that indiscriminate spraying creates an air quality problem for everyone within whiffing distance.

For your marriage to thrive and grow, it needs plenty of fresh air. The rude aroma of meanness, bad manners, and disrespect will always lead you in the wrong direction and take you off the road of love. Rudeness always leads husbands and wives away from one another into the reeking bogs of wounding words and distancing reactions. Has your husband or wife been pulling away from you lately? Do they seem distant or withdrawn? Have you considered that maybe nobody wants to hug a skunk?

James says that we all stumble in many ways, and it all begins with that little wet muscle that can be cracked like a whip. A snappy, unbridled tongue is a dead giveaway of conditional love. If you and I were never at fault with what we say, James writes, we would be perfect. A perfect tongue would keep us high on the mountain peaks of boundless love, above the mere mortals in the valley below who wrestle with impulsivity and self-restraint. Wouldn't that be perfect?

But as James and you and I well know, we're not perfect. Most of us didn't go to finishing school or attend the Emily Post Etiquette Institute. "Please," "Thank you," and "No, you go first, I insist" sound pleasant and refreshing, but in our weaker moments, we are steered by that small, fire-breathing appendage in our mouths that is capable of torching trees.

James doesn't mince words when he describes the power of the tongue. You may think he's rude for being so blunt, but he's telling it like it is. The tongue is a restless evil. A nasty, restless evil that relies on rudeness to bite back, cut down, lash out, and tear apart. Jesus said it himself: "For out of the overflow of the heart the mouth speaks" (Matt. 12:34). By helping us to understand how tongue-tied we are to rudeness, James hopes to steer us in the right direction.

> When we put bits into the mouths of horses to make them obey us, we can turn the whole animal. Or take ships as an example. Although they are so large and are driven by strong winds, they are steered by a very small rudder wherever the pilot wants to go. Likewise the tongue is a small part of the body, but it makes great boasts. Consider what a great forest is set on fire by a small spark. The tongue also is a fire, a world of evil among the parts of the body. It corrupts the whole person, sets the whole course of his life on fire, and is itself set on fire by hell.
>
> All kinds of animals, birds, reptiles and creatures of the sea are being tamed and have been tamed by man, but no man can tame the tongue. It is a restless evil, full of deadly poison.
>
> *James 3:3–8*

Ouch! According to James, we are the pilots of our tongues, and our tongues will go wherever we steer them. The resort town of Rudeness is a lonely vacation spot, and there's no lighthouse to lead the way. You want to pull into the Port of Profanity? You're the captain. Full steam ahead. You want to dock at the town of Disrespect? You're the skipper.

Proverbs 18:21 says, "Death and life are in the power of the tongue, and those who love it will eat its fruit" (NASB). We set our course with our choices, and our choices reveal the condition of our hearts. How does that rudder in your mouth steer your words? When you are in a conflict with your husband or wife, in what direction do you head? Do you steer toward love? Or is your rudder pointed on the path to rudeness? No one makes us say anything. Death and life are in the power of the tongue, and we get to choose the fragrance we deliver.

147

I'll never forget the time when Krista and I were out with a group of other couples and the wife of one man began to lay into him like a drill sergeant. Her comments were smelly, mean, and nasty. To his credit, the man chose the higher road. The path of love. He didn't strike back and slay with the sword of his tongue. (And in case you're wondering, this guy's not a wimp or a wuss.) His wife was dropping verbal cluster bombs, but he chose not to escalate the conflict by swinging below the belt.

The whole incident was embarrassing and awkward. I wanted to react. One more nasty comment and I was ready to pour my soda over this woman's head. Okay, that's a bit extreme. At least smashing my bean burrito in her face wouldn't stain her blouse.

It doesn't matter who's on the receiving end; it's a terrible thing to see a man verbally castrated by his wife or a woman be the target of her husband's unkind words in front of others.

We don't always get it right, but one thing Krista and I try to do when we're out for the evening or with family and friends is to be supportive and polite to one another in public. If there's a difference of opinion, a disagreement, or the subtle scent of an argument brewing, we try to save it for later when we get home. Rude in private is bad enough. Rudeness in public is Doheny Beach sanitation plant material.

> We set our course with our choices, and our choices reveal the condition of our hearts.

Rudeness always makes withdrawals, and this is where marriages get in trouble. When I sit with couples in counseling, it's often because rudeness is ruling over love. If you and I aren't careful, insensitivity and careless comments can quickly add up to an overdrawn account. This is when, on days when I'm tired or frustrated, my love looks more like fee-based banking than a fragrant bunch of sweet peas. Instead of making deposits that are free and unconditional, my conditional love is quite expensive. It costs Krista and our relationship a lot. Cross-eyed looks come with a $2 charge. A $1 fee is imposed when Krista forgets to pick up my clothes at the cleaners. A long honey-do list costs a stiff $10. These are the days when I feel whooped and downright stingy with my love. The only fragrance that lingers in my life is the rank odor of rudeness. The only thing I'm serving is half-baked leftovers of cold conditional love. I don't know why, but Krista doesn't like my leftovers.

Instead of spreading the fragrance of love around your home, are you banking on your spouse to make more deposits than you do? Do you mope through your evenings or weekends with poor customer service? Do you respond to a request or favor like everything's a chore? When asked to help with dinner, do you act like an insolent teenager taking orders at Taco Bell? Dude, is your love rude? Or maybe you've been the recipient of rudeness? Whether you're the rude reactor or rude recipient, there is a better choice. A more excellent way. Listen to these words of wisdom written long ago . . .

The more we allow love to enter, the more we grow to love others with our whole will—even when they treat us miserably. In fact, God's aim is to change us from within so that it is the easiest thing for us to act in love at these times, whether we are overwhelmed with feeling or not. Speaking and responding in love is most precious, because that's when we are fully open to God, obeying an action that originated in His heart. This is how His Spirit continually flows into this world—*through us*—to overcome the world's meanness. I tell you, acting in love when others are not acting in love toward you—this is of the highest value to your soul. It is worth more than all the other works of faith you may have done, no matter how great they appear. Love is the highest aim, the greatest practice you can cultivate in your soul. It is the path on which you walk as closely as possible to those who are already living in the life eternal.[4]

So how do you rise above the smell of rudeness? How do you counter the way of this world's meanness? How can you move from being one who trades a curse for a curse to being one who knows how to steer your tongue in the right direction? If you feel whipped from hurtful words and discouraged by your spouse's lack of kindness, the best place to start is by digging into the Gospels and reading about the rudeness Jesus encountered as he wandered from town to town. You'll find a friend to walk with as you discover a more excellent way to love.

You see, if there's anyone who understands how to repel odious and boorish behavior, it's Jesus. Christ had to put up with so many rude people; it's amazing he never pulled the plug on Palestine. But the Jesus of the Bible never demonstrated an unconditional love like a soft, absorbent sponge that soaked up every wrong and never stood up for itself. Search the Scriptures and you won't find a spineless, flannel-graph Jesus who got walked on as the world's doormat.

The person you'll encounter is the Jesus who stilled storms and walked on water. You'll duck for cover when you see the whip-cracking, table-turning, make-a-mess-of-everything Messiah in the temple courts. You'll be encouraged to discover that real unconditional love comes from the One who told us to be innocent as doves and shrewd as snakes. Walk alongside Jesus, and you'll discover what he does with rude. His Spirit will give you a new perspective, another viewpoint, a way out of rudeness by choosing the way of love. The writer of Hebrews tells us to "fix our eyes on Jesus, the author and perfecter of our faith" and to "consider him who endured such opposition from sinful men, so that you will not grow weary and lose heart" (Heb. 12:2–3). As if it wasn't enough just to hang innocent on a cross, Jesus had to endure these noxious taunts flung his way . . .

"Those who passed by hurled insults at him, shaking their heads" (Matt. 27:39).

"In the same way the robbers who were crucified with him also heaped insults on him" (Matt. 27:44).

"The people stood watching, and the rulers even sneered at him. They said, 'He saved others; let him save himself if he is the Christ of God, the Chosen One.' The soldiers also came up and mocked him" (Luke 23:35–36).

Name calling. Insults. Challenges. Accusations. Lies. Mocking abuse hurled and heaped on him by sinners, soldiers, and robbers that goes beyond the pale of rudeness. This is the one who bore our sins. He endured pain and suffering so that in our pain and suffering we might be transformed by his love that can bear all things.

In similar fashion, Paul endured harsh treatment, but as a man transformed by the love of God, he chose the way of love. Calling himself a fool for Christ, which made him a fool for love, he wrote to the Corinthians about the rude treatment he received:

> Paul was treated like trash, like the refuse of the world, but he chose to spread a different kind of fragrance. A fragrance this world will never understand.

To this very hour we go hungry and thirsty, we are in rags, we are brutally treated, we are homeless. We work hard with our own hands. When we are cursed, we bless; when we are persecuted, we endure it; when we are slandered, we answer kindly. Up to this moment we have become the scum of the earth, the refuse of the world.

1 Corinthians 4:11–13

Paul was treated like trash, like the refuse of the world, but he chose to spread a different kind of fragrance. A fragrance this world will never understand. Despite all the challenges and difficulties he encountered, Paul was able to keep his eyes fixed on Jesus and be thankful to God, who "through us spreads everywhere the fragrance of the knowledge of him" (2 Cor. 2:14). We are the aroma of Christ. Whether we realize it or not, we emit a fragrance as we enter a room, and we leave a fragrance behind after we leave. If you keep meandering through the New Testament, you'll discover a whole arsenal of odor repellents that come directly from the grace of God to help us live with a more excellent love. These are the choices within your grasp and mine . . .

"Be kind and compassionate to one another, forgiving each other, just as in Christ God forgave you" (Eph. 4:32).

"Therefore encourage one another and build each other up" (1 Thess. 5:11).

"And let us consider how we may spur one another on toward love and good deeds" (Heb. 10:24).

"Love one another deeply, from the heart" (1 Peter 1:22).

"Greet one another with a kiss of love" (1 Peter 5:14).

If Paul were here, he just might ask you and me: "What kind of aroma are you giving off? Are you attracting or repelling? Are you lighting candles of love to dispel the smell of rudeness?"

When I write, I like to light a scented candle to fill my office with a relaxing aroma. I don't know much about aromatherapy, but I do know the difference between what smells good and what doesn't. I know what kind of comments make sweet-pea deposits and what kind makes rude withdrawals. I know enough to remember that *love is not rude*. It is courteous and considerate and polite. It thinks of others and is filled with grace. It is not blunt or brutal. It never seeks to damage another. Love chooses its words wisely and seeks forgiveness when acting like a chump or a chumpette.

As the God of all love, our heavenly Father never uses his power in a rude or unbecoming way. His love always leads you and me in the right direction. Leave yourself time in your day to linger over his love letter to you, and he will direct your steps. And then, after you have meandered and meditated through the pages of Scripture in pursuit of his love for you, go find that wedding video of yours. Pop it in for a few minutes and watch that special day, when you knew exactly how to treat one another with the utmost honor and respect. Nobody had to tell you—you knew how to act as a groom. You didn't need any coaching—you knew the graceful manner of a bride. As you walked down the aisle, you both began the journey of marriage, promising to love and honor one another for the rest of your lives. It's a road that's still worth walking.

So keep your eyes on Jesus through the valley as you push on toward the peaks. Don't forget to stop beyond the next hillside to pick some sweet peas. Go ahead and pick a big bunch for one another. This year's bloom is incredible. *They smell so good.*

And while you're picking, how about a little love in the afternoon?

> As the God of all love, our heavenly Father never uses his power in a rude or unbecoming way. His love always leads you and me in the right direction.

CHAPTER TWELVE

He-Mail, She-Mail

It is the entirely unselfish nature of God's love that seeks our own good. In loving us, God does not seek his own praise, honor, profit, or pleasure. He loves us because it is his nature to love us.

Working out of my home office has all sorts of perks. Though navigating my way through the congested traffic of errant toys and disembodied clothes down the hallway to my upstairs office is probably one of the most dangerous commutes in Orange County, I am saving money on gas. Where I work, the coffee is really good. French roast. But it's self-service with a smile. I have yet to install a water cooler, because there's no one to talk to, so I talk to my plants (which is supposed to be good for the plants, but it's actually making my wife very concerned about my psychological need to be around people). And there's never a line for the bathroom, although having other people in the bathroom right next to my office can be pretty embarrassing. One time I was on the phone with my publisher, and Ellie screamed from where she sat on the potty, "Daddy! Come wipe me!"

I work in a very professional corporate environment.

By far the greatest perk of working out of my home office is, well, um . . . how do I put this delicately . . . is a little lovin' in the afternoon with my wife when the kids are at school. Working at home is *great*. A definite way to spice up our love life, though I think it's driving Krista crazy.

I don't know about you, but by the time we get our four kids to bed, we're exhausted. Completely pooped. You moms know, when you're absolutely physically and emotionally drained from kids nipping at your ankles all day, the last thing you want is your husband to become Don Rico Suave at 11:00 at night.

But we guys, we have needs. Deep emotional needs. Don't we? We want to bond. Connect. We need to be held. We need to be cherished. That's why we need sex—this is how these deep emotional needs are met. Which is why I think my "love needs" are driving Krista crazy when she comes home after a morning of playing tennis.

My take on sex and the work-at-home situation is simple. The kids aren't home. We're wide awake. Let's shun housework and get to the real work of a little lovin' in the afternoon. Oh yeah, baby. If we have time, energy, and opportunity, why not? To which Krista would rebut, "Time, energy, and opportunity do not necessarily motivate me to want to make love. You're going to have to do better than that."

There's that conditional *do* word. Love for performance. Jump through the hoop. You want love in the afternoon, it's going to cost you. Though I am in the midst of writing a book on unconditional love, I am saddened to say that I'm married to a woman who sees life through a very conditional paradigm of life. Which isn't such a bad thing. The key issue here is not lack of desire but motivation. Men like a challenge, so my task is to discover what motivates my wife.

155

Last week when Krista came home from tennis, I was in the mood for love. A perfect opportunity to motivate her like a Zig Ziglar sales conference (and my best writing ideas come from maximizing such motivational moments). Krista happened to be in the shower when I crooned from the bathroom door in my best Dean Martin voice, "I'm in the mood for love."

"Ugh," Krista groaned. "I knew you were going to say that."

"That's right," I said in the best motivational voice I could muster. "Nobody's home, so let's seize the day!"

"You go seize the day and finish that book. Get back to work. I'm taking a shower."

"I'll take one with you."

"No!"

At this point, my motivational message was dissipating faster than the steam in the shower. I resorted to blatant exaggeration based on my current emotional need.

"It's been years since we made love."

"Fix my e-mail."

"What?" I said, not sure where she was heading with this command.

"You fix my e-mail, and we'll make love."

"That's scandalous. Outright sexual extortion. That's pay for performance."

"That's right. Fix my e-mail."

Krista knew she had me, and I now knew what motivated her. For the past week, her e-mail had been down, and I'd spent forty minutes the night before trying to fix it. But Krista didn't marry Microsoft tech support; I couldn't get it to work. And now I was going to be losing out on love in the afternoon because of my poor performance.

"That's not fair. I spent almost an hour last night trying to fix your e-mail. I have no idea what's wrong with it."

"You want lovin' in the afternoon, fix my e-mail."

I've always liked a woman who knows what she wants.

I dashed out of the bathroom and down the hallway, leaping over toys, clothes, and tall buildings in a single bound. I fired up her computer and opened her Outlook e-mail program. I was a man on a mission. A she-mail mission of love.

I clicked through a number of different screens and brought up her e-mail user account, going through exactly the same steps I did the night before. Hoping against all hope, I deleted her user profile and created a new one. New name. New password. New everything. Anything for love in the afternoon, right?

I zipped back to the desktop and clicked open Internet Explorer, logging into our Internet account. I updated Krista's new e-mail settings and said to myself, "Come on, come on, this has gotta work." At this point, the whole scenario looked very iffy to me. I had done these exact same steps the night before and nothing had worked. I closed Explorer and went back to Outlook. I closed her new account settings, went to her Inbox, and clicked the Send/Receive button.

"Come on, baby. Come to Papa."

Ding, ding, ding, ding!

Four new e-mails jumped into Krista's Inbox. *Yes!*

I whooped and hollered. "I did it! I did it! It works!"

I now knew how Tom Edison felt when that lightbulb popped on the very first time. I now knew the elation Alexander Graham Bell experienced when he heard Mr. Watson on the other line. I now knew how Wilbur and Orville Wright felt while flying their first plane. I ran back down the hallway screaming like a madman in a crazy, chanting voice.

"I fixed your e-mail. I fixed your e-mail."

"No way," Krista said, caught off guard, with a look of "what have I gotten myself into" on her face.

"And you owe me big time! Because I'm Mr. She-mail." I pointed at myself and then to Krista, "He-mail . . . she-mail! It's time for a little lovin' in the afternoon!" Strutting like a rooster in the chicken coop, I preened and danced through our bedroom to the laughter and angst of my wife. Who says computer nerds can't be sexy?

Now I already know what you're thinking. If you're a guy reading this, you're slapping me a high five like I just bagged a three-pointer at the buzzer. Men love a challenge, and I'd just conquered the Mt. Everest of e-mail challenges. If you're a female/she-mail reading this, you're probably appalled at such self-congratulatory behavior and the bravado I brought to my technological conquest. If I may plead my case for a moment, I wasn't the one who set the conditions. Krista did. With her one condition, she became this book's poster child. No unconditional love. Only a she-mail condition. Shameless, absolutely shameless.

As a result of my superior tech-support performance, I informed Krista that her pay-for-performance "condition" was definite writing material for the book you now have in your hands. She deadpanned, "I'm glad I could be of service to you."

The pleasure was mine. All mine in a self-seeking sort of way. I'm not sure this is what Paul had in mind when he said that love is not self-seeking. He didn't have the benefit of e-mail or the Internet to broadcast God's message of unconditional love to the world, but given the time and place where Paul lived, he didn't need any high-tech assistance to deliver his message. He had something better: the presence of the Holy Spirit in his heart and the proof of his own transformed life. Before Paul had come face to face with God's unconditional love, he'd sought his own glory and honor by imprisoning the early Christians. He was a self-seeker. Definitely not a God-seeker. Little did he know God was seeking him on the road to Damascus.

When you begin to realize that God actively seeks you out, and when you choose to respond to the unconditional, transforming love of God, there is nothing you can do but come away a transformed person. This is exactly what happened to Paul. His life was now no longer solely about himself. His life wasn't about what he wanted; it was about pursuing the will of God and living in gratitude by serving others. Paul's new spiritual identity, how he understood himself as a child of God, was to follow in Jesus' footsteps and live as Christ himself lived as a servant to all.

When Krista asked me to fix her e-mail, she had her one condition, but was there any hint of self-seeking motivation on my part? You bet there was. I was seeking love in the after-noon—a perfectly reasonable expectation of sexual intimacy between a husband and a wife—but was my highest motivation to serve Krista or myself? Me again. More often than not, my motives are self-seeking and self-serving. Sometimes I'm not motivated by unconditional love but by the conditions in my heart that want what they want.

To Paul, the new standard of loving God is service, the mea-sure of spiritual greatness set by Jesus for all of his followers. Not self-service. True love does not seek its own needs first. True, authentic love seeks to serve the needs of others first. That's a tall order.

Even the disciples had a hard time with this one. Though they were being served daily by the Son of God, they weren't always the sharpest crayons in the box. When James and John asked Jesus for first dibs to sit at his right and left in his kingdom, these two aspiring teacher's pets started a near riot among the other guys, who were now angry and saying to one another, "Hey, why didn't we think of that first?" It was ten disciples against two when Jesus got into the middle of the fray. "Whoever wants to become great among you must be your servant, and whoever wants to be first must be slave of all. For even the Son of Man did not come to be served, but to serve, and to give his life as a ransom for many" (Mark 10:43–45).

> True love does not seek its own needs first.

159

Self-imposed slavery—being the servant of all—doesn't go over too well in our individualistic, self-serving society. However, serving your husband, your wife, or others does not mean you can't acknowledge your own needs. Most of us are well aware of the conditional love we experienced in the past when we didn't have some of our basic emotional needs met. This is why one of the greatest fears in relationships is not having our deepest needs for love and acceptance met.

Paul is not asking us to abandon or deny our needs, because every person has very real and significant emotional, spiritual, physical, sexual, and relational needs. But living in a self-serving way is no way to get what we really want and need. True love does not seek its own. Adult relationships, marriage in particular, are mutual relationships, in which a man and woman choose to serve one another in love.

Our personhood, which includes those needs that make up part of who we uniquely are, is what distinguishes us from the personhood of another. God wired us to have these needs met in mutual, life-giving relationships. We are made to seek one another out. The one condition, the key condition, Paul asks us to consider as husbands and wives is that we be motivated to meet one another's needs with a mutual, self-giving love. Paul put it this way:

> Do nothing out of selfish ambition or vain conceit, but in humility consider others better than yourselves. Each of you should look not only to your own interests, but also to the interests of others.
>
> Your attitude should be the same as that of Christ Jesus:
>
> Who being in very nature God,
> > did not consider equality with God something to be grasped,
> but made himself nothing,
> > taking the very nature of a servant,

being made in human likeness.
And being found in appearance as a man,
    he humbled himself
    and became obedient to death—even death on a cross!

Philippians 2:3–8

Marriage is a continual dance between understanding and meeting one another's wants, needs, expectations, and desires. Paul calls us to choose and follow the most excellent way of love, to do nothing out of self-seeking ambition or vain e-mail-conquering conceit but to humbly consider others better than ourselves. Since marriage is also a relationship marked by tension, because these normal and natural needs don't always align themselves like we would like them to, Paul tells us to take on Jesus' attitude in serving each other. If the God of this universe could take on the very nature of a servant, isn't it possible for him to give us the power and strength to serve one another before ourselves?

Through the different and changing seasons of married life here in the valley, we are not always good at guessing what our spouses want or need at any given time. Nor are our spouses necessarily good at reading our hearts and minds in determining our particular wants and needs. This is why we need the others-centered attitude of Christ. We get stuck in our marriages when the pursuit of our own wants and needs supercedes our choice to willingly

> If the God of this universe could take on the very nature of a servant, isn't it possible for him to give us the power and strength to serve one another before ourselves?

161

seek the good of our spouses. When we hunker down and turn inward by grabbing whatever we can for ourselves, we are no longer motivated by love but instead by a self-seeking attitude of the heart filled with conditional love.

I love what Matthew Henry wrote about the unselfish nature of God's love, or "charity" as it was called long ago.

> Charity is an utter enemy to selfishness; it does not desire or seek its own praise, or honor, or profit, or pleasure. Not that charity destroys all regard to ourselves, or that the charitable man should neglect himself and all his interests. But charity never seeks its own to the hurt of others, or to neglect others.[5]

It is the entirely unselfish nature of God's love that seeks our own good. In loving us, as Matthew Henry writes, God does not seek his own praise, honor, profit, or pleasure. He loves us because it is his nature. It's a wonderful thought to consider that God cannot *not* love us. God is love and he cannot deny his very nature. In not denying himself, he freely gives us what we do not deserve. He freely gives us what we do not seek. Even when we are self-seeking, God seeks us out to show us a more excellent way. That is the excellent nature of his love.

As much as we'd like to be more loving and less self-seeking, every marriage gets stuck in the weeds. When a couple comes to me for marriage counseling, we'll sit down and I'll listen to the grocery list of grievances they have with one another. *He doesn't help put the kids to bed. She complains about my schedule. He expects me to bring in the trash cans. She gets way more playtime than I do.* On rare occasions of deep psychological and spiritual insight, I might say, "It sounds like both of you are acting pretty selfish." On more occasions than not, the couple looks at each other, then at me, and says, "You're right."

And who isn't? What person, what couple, isn't selfish? When I'm lying on the couch reading a good book, it's so easy for me to say to Krista or one of the kids, "Hey, could you get me something to drink?" But do I respond to their requests to help them out when asked? Sometimes yes. Sometimes no. Selfishness is a shortcut to spiritual and marital growth, and sometimes the longest distance between two points is a shortcut.

Just this morning, I went out to get the paper and noticed the front tire was low on our minivan. I walked inside the house and told Krista her car tire needed air and to be sure to get some today. She replied that she had a long list of things to do and asked if we could switch cars so I could get air in the tire.

"Me? Put air in your tire? I can't because I've also got a lot of things to do today. It'll only take you a couple minutes. No big deal."

That was my response. Perfectly logical. Joe Friday just stating the facts. And entirely self-seeking, because when it really comes down to it, I don't like driving the minivan. I'd rather drive my manlier Ford Expedition, because I don't want to look like a minivan mom (now I'm exposing my deeper vanity and utter lack of humility). I also didn't want to be inconvenienced. I didn't want to stop for two minutes to get air in the tire. I didn't want to think about serving Krista. I was seeking what was best for me, me, and me. I knew what the most excellent way was, but I struggled with the choice.

You and I cannot live an others-centered life apart from remaining in the transforming love of Jesus. Because of the brokenness in our lives, we will always default to preserving and protecting our own special interests. We are consummate self-seeking lobbyists for our own agendas. The multitude of conditions in our hearts is wired to ask what's in it for us. Following

> Selfishness is a shortcut to spiritual and marital growth, and we all know that the longest distance between two points is a shortcut.

Jesus through the valley of our lives is an ever-changing process of seeking to become more like him as we learn to choose the way of love and serve others as he did. The way of Jesus is the way of love, and service is the clear demonstration of a heart set on fire by the love of God.

Seeking the good of our spouses is usually found in the little things of life. It's the simple acts of love and kindness that express our interest and concern for one another. That's where true love makes the biggest difference. In the little things of life, like letting our wife sleep in while we take the kids out for donuts on Saturday morning. Or like making a fresh pot of coffee and serving it up just like our husband likes it. It's seeking this higher way of serving, the most excellent way of love we have to offer our spouses. In giving of ourselves, we take on the attitude of Christ and become more like him. In seeking the good of each other, we just might lose some of those life-limiting conditions in our hearts and develop a deeper love for one another along the way.

Even if that means we have to stop and get air in the tire.

Two minutes out of my day is not worth getting angry over.

CHAPTER THIRTEEN

Anger Mismanagement

I don't think many Christians really know what to do with an angry Jesus. It completely implodes our unspoken preference for a passive, flannel-graph Jesus.

This is the class no one wants to sign up for. In the front row slouches a large, leather-vested biker. Ever since getting off Jenny Craig last year, he hasn't been a happy camper, but the rage inside him goes deeper than that. Much deeper. Can barely squeeze himself into his desk, but I wouldn't say anything if I were you. Last month's bar fight garnered him free enrollment here in the state-sponsored Anger Management 101. The judge offered him a yearlong opportunity to take a long, hard look at himself and what makes him tick. Or should we say, ticked off? It's either that or ninety days in jail.

Then there's the doctor. Clean-cut but smirking. His arrogance precedes him. He thinks he's different. Special. Not like the lowlifes surrounding him. The doctor is tan and athletic, but he has a thing or two to learn about good sportsmanship. He hasn't learned that an overcooked steak doesn't give him the right to hit his wife with his tennis racket.

See the petite blonde in the corner? Scared as a mouse, isn't she? But her nervousness is nothing. You should see her children cower when she gets out the belt. The way she disciplines her children, her argument goes, can't compare with how her father beat her. The judge doesn't see it that way, but she does have a choice: a year of anger management or jail.

Then there's the guy over in the corner. Yeah, at the back of the class. Long hair. Beard. Rainbow sandals and Levis. Doesn't look particularly angry. Oh, he's the one. Thrashed the church downtown last week. I read about that one in the newspaper. Sounds like he caused quite a commotion. He's a ticked-off religious extremist, they say. Did you hear the same story I did?

I had a few friends who saw the whole thing. It was business as usual in the temple courts. People were buying and selling like they always do. The place was packed. The price for sacrificial offerings had skyrocketed over the past few years, but business is business, right? And the money changers, those guys were making money hand over fist. Anyone from out of town got nailed. Exchange rates were absolutely unconscionable.

From what I heard, everybody was cutting deals and minding their own business when this guy showed up. I think his name is Jesus. Yeah, the same guy who made a big splash coming into Jerusalem on a donkey the other day. Anyway, this Jesus was strolling through the temple courts, looking at all the merchandise, scoping out what was going on. He was from out of town and had a bunch of buddies with him. No one was paying much attention, when all of a sudden he unleashed an incredible roar as loud and ferocious as a lion. Heads spun, and before anyone could do anything, this Jesus dumped a table loaded with money and weights and scales. Of course the owner of the table was screaming and diving for his money. Coins scattered and rolled across the floor in every direction. A piggy bank could have minimized his losses.

This guy from Galilee didn't stop there. He ran from table to table, flipping them like hotcakes. Scales crashed to the ground. People were jumping out of the way. No one bothered to stop him, because everyone was on their hands and knees, scooping up as much money as they could. Jesus must have knocked over ten to fifteen tables before sending an entire ATM machine crashing down a flight of stairs. People were yelling. Some were cheering. International currency, coins from all over the world, were mixed and scattered all over the place. Nobody knew who owned what or how much.

If that weren't enough, not only did Jesus trash the place, he then grabbed a bunch of electrical cords and made a whip like he was the new sheriff in town. He was swinging it over his head and yelling something about all the buyers and sellers making his Father's house the OK Corral. He ran over to the animal stalls. He opened the gates, cracked his whip, and incited a stampede. Cattle and sheep and goats were mooing and bleating in the mayhem. Jesus flipped open the dove cages, and it was like someone had broke open Noah's ark. The kids loved it, but their parents were panicked, scooping them up left and right. The kids, that is. It's all fun and games until someone gets hurt.

Jesus didn't stop. He began chucking benches left and right. "You should've seen the look in this Jesus' eyes," my buddies told me. "You do not want to mess with this guy." A definite anger problem. By the time the temple police showed up, it was too late. The damage had already been done. On his way out, Jesus ducked out through the crowds, yelling something about making his Father's house a den of robbers and turning the temple into a Target.

Who does this guy think he is? God?

In today's world, Jesus' temple redecorating riot definitely would have booked him a one-way ticket into an anger management class. But what if, as part of his class participation, Jesus was actually asked to teach the class? Maybe write a small research paper to make him reflect on what he'd just done? Prepare a little lesson about anger mismanagement? What would Jesus have to say about anger?

He'd have absolutely no problem preparing the curriculum. He has lots of material to draw on, doesn't he? Though placed in an anger management class for all the wrong reasons, Jesus could set the record straight by clearing up a lot of confusion on the most volatile of emotions. If we were sitting in the class, right away he'd grab a dry-erase pen and write on the board that love is not easily angered. He wouldn't say that anger is a sin. It's not. He'd write up on the board in big, bold letters: ANGER IS AN EMOTION . . . USE IT BEFORE YOU LOSE IT.

Anger is a powerful force that can propel transformation and positive change. Jesus probably would also tell the class that anger is a part of every marriage and every relationship. But tapping on the board, he'd emphasize his main point again, that love is not easily angered. Easing his way through his material, Jesus would point out the relational fallacies and confusing ideas people have about anger; stuff you and I read about in greeting cards and see on bumper stickers. Spoken and unspoken ideas people live by: "Love means never having to say you're sorry." "We never get angry at one another; we love each other." "If I get angry, my spouse won't love me or like me." "Anger is wrong." His personal favorite bumper sticker? "Jesus Is Coming Back and Boy Is He Ticked!"

Jesus would certainly have your attention by now. He is a captivating teacher, you know. He'd look you in the eye and tell you that no one is responsible for your anger but you. No matter what your past or family history or what you've been through, reality is all about now, and you have the choice of how to handle your anger. Though he did turn over more than a few tables, Jesus would say that your anger gives you no right to hit or hurt anyone. You're not above the law of the land or the law of God. He'd say that not even he's above the law, but rather, he came to fulfill the law, the law of love. Then he'd point back to the white board and, like any good teacher, emphasize his point again: Love is not easily angered.

I'm sure he'd have a few good quotes about what others have said about anger. He'd point to some of the truths about anger in these words . . .

Never lose your temper, except intentionally.

Dwight D. Eisenhower

When angry, count to ten before you speak; if very angry, a hundred.

Thomas Jefferson

Anger makes you smaller, while forgiveness forces you to grow beyond what you were.

Cherie Carter-Scott

Anger is a signal, and one worth listening to.
Harriet Lerner

The voice of honest indignation is the voice of God.

William Blake

As he reads this last quote to the class from the podium, his eyes light up. God, his Father, is one of Jesus' favorite persons to talk about. Looking for a show of hands, Jesus asks the class, "How many of you get angry when someone breaks a promise to you?" A few tentative hands go up. "How many of you don't like it when someone doesn't keep their word?" A

169

couple more. "How many of you like repeating the same thing over and over again, hoping for change, but all of your words seem to fall on deaf ears?" This one hits a nerve. A bunch more hands go up.

"Tell me now," Jesus says slowly, "how you think God might feel when people break his laws that are written for their own good? How does God feel when people don't keep their promises to him? What's going on inside God's heart when his people, his beloved, run off with other lovers? What if someone walked into your Father's house and set up a spiritual sweatshop? A covenant-breaking corporate scandal? A house of prayer that priced people out of the market? What would you feel?"

Everyone's eyes are riveted on Jesus. People lean forward in their seats and blurt out their responses.

"Angry!"

"Jealous!"

"Betrayed!"

"Rejected!"

"Abandoned!"

"Ripped off and ticked off."

"You got that right," Jesus says as he points to the fat biker. "That's exactly what I feel when you reject me. I feel incensed. No, that's too weak . . . enraged when you run off with other lovers." He's pointing to all of us in the class now. "That's the burning anger, the jealousy I feel inside, but my love is deeper than a feeling. My love for you is greater than my anger. Have you not read Psalm 86:15: 'But you, O LORD, are a compassionate and gracious God, slow to anger, abounding in love and faithfulness'?"

Jesus taps on the white board one more time. The entire room is silent. In a whisper, Jesus says, "Don't you get it? Don't you understand my love for you? Repeat this with me . . . my love is not easily angered."

Do you need to spend some time in class with Jesus? I know I don't think enough about how some of my choices make him feel. I've broken more promises to him than I can count, but I have discovered that his love is not easily angered. It's the same love Paul discovered when he got flicked off his horse on the way to Damascus. For every crime and atrocity Paul committed, did Jesus punish Paul as his crimes deserved? If Jesus were really angry at Paul, think of everything he could have done to him. Pulverize. Vaporize. Liquefy. Jesus doesn't treat us as our sins deserve, but in his mercy, he relents in favor of love.

Jesus is the best anger management teacher you and I could ever have. No one better knows how to walk that fine line between righteous, godly anger and the destructive, sin-soaked anger that gets us in trouble. Could Jesus be described as anything less than passionate? Wasn't Jesus known for strong feelings and definite opinions? He comes from a lineage of kings, the royal line of David, but was his anger ever not righteous? Not justified? Does Jesus use his anger to throttle people? Is this the same Jesus who said, "But I tell you that anyone who is angry with his brother will be subject to judgment," but who said to Peter, "Get behind me, Satan!" Strong words from a friend and Savior. Angry, yes, but righteous.

But we don't do anger real well, do we? Here in the valley, we go to extremes. Sometimes we stuff our anger down inside of us. We may have had a mother or father who unloaded on us with explosive anger, so we've just told ourselves we don't get angry. We minimize our long list of annoyances. Suck up our resentments. Pretend we're fine. Put on a plastic smile. And then we fib.

> Jesus is the best anger management teacher you and I could ever have.

I'm not mad, just hurt.
Liar.

Instead of being honest with our emotions and opening a vent for frank conversation, we pack down our anger, wrap it in razor wire, and lightly dangle a finger before our hair-trigger hearts.

Others of us keep our anger close to the surface of every little problem, conflict, and obstacle we encounter throughout our day. We're like fragmentation mines, Bouncing Betties is what they called them in Vietnam, that are triggered whenever someone applies a little pressure or trips our wires. We jump three feet out of the ground, bursting our invective in a deadly, 360-degree spray of shrapnel. The only part of our hearts that we dare expose to our spouses is a small fuse.

Jan Johnson wrote,

> Pretending not to be angry does not work. Angry feelings get buried alive and leak out in grumbling, sarcasm, cynicism, or stubbornness. Anger turned inward becomes depression, and concealed anger betrays its presence in passive aggressive behaviors such as chronic lateness. Some of us "use" buried anger to become high achievers so we can prove ourselves to those who doubt us. Or we withdraw, saying "I'm not mad. I'm just outta here." Unexamined, anger takes on a life of its own within us.[6]

That Jan Johnson makes me so mad. She completely exposes my tendency to stuff my own anger. In my own life and marriage, I have the tendency to stuff my anger out of fear that if I really let it fly, I might face rejection from Krista. And so my thinking goes (and there are many times I don't even know I'm thinking this way), why not just stuff it and keep the peace even though it's a superficial level of peace and not the deep intimacy that can result from new understandings that come from difficult conflicts. A lot of times, I don't even know I'm angry, but my anger comes out in moodiness or irritability or in my snapper-turtle tendencies. Now, when I know I'm angry about something, I try to say how I feel by letting Krista know where I am on my emotional radar screen. Something clear and to the point like . . .

"I'm angry!"

Inevitably, Krista comes back and lets me know where she is on her emotional radar screen. Something clear and to the point like . . .

"Well, this makes me angry too!"

Now all cards are on the table, and we both have some meaty visceral emotions to work with instead of playing guessing games or emotional Wheel of Fortune. Stuffing anger does not work. Read that again. Emotional intimacy comes from vulnerability, and that sometimes requires the courageous act of honestly dealing with our anger for what it is.

If Paul were sitting down with us right now, he'd offer us a new perspective. A new life instead of an unexamined life of anger. He'd probably open the pages of Scripture to show us how much the Bible talks about anger. He'd help us get a realistic point of view, a right angle, on this powerful emotion. Like Jesus, he'd remind us love is not easily angered, but he might add that unconditional love gets ticked off about the right things. Let's take a closer look.

The Bible is a book filled with angry people. Plenty of people like you and me get miffed, lit, and irate in the Bible. Peeved at God and more than annoyed at one another. Lots of teeth gnashing. To name a few characters and unforgettable stories: Cain killed his brother with his anger. A drunk and naked Noah—yes, the Noah of children's Bible story fame—cursed his grandkids after Ham told his brothers that Dad was sleeping in the buff. When the Israelites worshipped the golden calf, Moses burned with so much anger that he slam-dunked the Ten Commandments right into the ground.

After Moses refused to listen to Joshua and Caleb about taking the Promised Land, was God not angry with the Israelites for forty years? When his people flagrantly disobeyed or complained about the poor dining conditions in the desert, didn't God occasionally have the ground swallow 'em up or send in venomous snakes to bite the whiners? How many times did Moses have to remind the Israelites, "I told you he was a jealous God; you do not want to tick him off"?

The Bible is a book filled with angry people. Plenty of people like you and me get miffed, lit, and irate in the Bible. Peeved at God and more than annoyed at one another. Lots of teeth gnashing.

In the New Testament, a man planning a great banquet became infuriated when his servant told him that none of his invited guests planned on coming to the party. The servant rattled off all the excuses of the invited guests: Busy at the office and can't get away. Shopping for the latest in longhorn cattle. Just got married. "Fine," the angry master said. "We redo the guest list." (What I like most about the kingdom of God are all the parties. God is quite the partier.)

In another party scene, the prodigal's older brother got so ticked off that he refused to enter a party hosted by his father for his dimwit brother who just blew half the family fortune. And the Pharisees got more than hot under the collar when Jesus healed on the Sabbath. If Jesus knew healing people on the Sabbath ticked the Pharisees off, why'd he keep doing it? Was it Jesus' fault for "making" the Pharisees angry? Jesus throws it back in their face: "Guys! Guys! Guys! If you can snip a little bit of skin and circumcise on the Sabbath, why get angry with me for healing the whole man on the Sabbath?" That is not what they wanted to hear.

I don't think many Christians really know what to do with an angry Jesus. It completely implodes our unspoken preference for a passive, flannel-graph Jesus. We'd rather send him to an anger management class than deal with the truth that, unlike him, we stuff our anger or resort to mean, destructive anger. If we're really serious about growing in unconditional love, that means we have to examine how our conditional love is played out in unresolved anger issues. Looking at Jesus, following Jesus, means looking at how we act in anger is so different from how he acts in anger. This is the hard work of spiritual transformation.

It'd be so much easier if we just had a declawed Jesus. An angry Jesus completely unravels our stereotypes and personal perceptions of how we see God. But if we'd see through the eyes of Scripture, we'd discover a Jesus who uses his unlimited power within limits. He exercises his almighty sovereignty and complete control over all of creation with self-control. His absolute authority and righteous anger are managed with loving restraint. In short, Jesus is not easily angered. He gets angry over the right things and upsets the apple cart when he sees the fruit of religious life filled with self-righteous worms. Jesus is honest and upfront with his anger. There is no halfheartedness or dishonesty or timid hand-wringing. What you see is what you get, which is maybe why Jesus tells us to become like little children.

You want to see honest anger? Try taking my three-year-old, Aidan, to swimming lessons. Hell hath no fury like a screaming boy dunked in a pool against his will. Nobody

> Jesus is not easily angered. He gets angry over the right things and upsets the apple cart when he sees the fruit of religious life filled with self-righteous worms.

175

had to teach Aidan the three Rs: Raging, Ranting, and Raving. I thought I saw hot lava pouring out his ears. By the time Aidan got out of the pool, there wasn't a drop of water left in it. Scalding anger plus hot-blooded fury equals evaporation. The thing about kids and anger, though, is that when they are angry, you know exactly where they're at. There's no pretending, hiding, sugarcoating, covering up, or acting like everything's fine. They are angry, and they want the world to know it. But as adults, dealing with our anger like Aidan just doesn't work.

So maybe it's time for us to go to school about our anger instead of stuffing it or resorting to destructive anger the moment someone does something we don't like. Maybe it's time to learn about what's really in our hearts instead of lashing out. Maybe it's time to seek understanding instead of unleashing the furies of hell.

As you can imagine, our friend Paul is ready and willing to help. Remember that when he wrote to the Corinthians, the church was filled with people who loved each other so much that they could never imagine hurting or getting angry at one another. Wrong. The Corinthian church, like any marriage or relationship, was filled with disagreements and clashes. In his second letter, even Paul was afraid of what he was going to find on his next visit to the Corinthian church. "I fear that there may be quarreling, jealousy, *outbursts of anger*, factions, slander, gossip, arrogance and disorder" (2 Cor. 12:20, emphasis added).

By reminding us that love is not easily angered, Paul's dropping a subtle hint that relationships aren't easy. Marriages are messy; they take work, and conflict is the anvil by which our disagreements are hammered out. Paul doesn't say love never gets angry, or love makes you the world's doormat to wipe its feet on, or love is always calm and perfectly gentle. It's okay to get angry; just do it in the right way. Like a watchful, protective guide, Paul points out the dangers of unrestrained anger. He told the people in the Ephesian church, "'In your anger do not sin.' Do not let the sun go down while you are still angry, and do not give the devil a foothold" (Eph. 4:26–27).

Giving full vent to anger is like a navy jet turning on the afterburners for a carrier landing. It's the wrong maneuver for landing on a small deck. Our anger may thrust an issue forward, but it's not worth it if we sin by severing relationships. If we stuff or minimize our anger by putting it to sleep for extended periods of time, we give the devil a boost into our brokenness. Instead of figuring out what we're angry about and taking steps to resolve it through counseling or a safe small group in our church, ignoring our anger creates footholds for our spiritual enemy to ease his way into our hearts. To the Colossians, Paul said to get rid of anything that hinted of the old, untransformed life. Anger. Rage. Malice. Slander. Filthy language.

Last, look at the Book of James: "My dear brothers, take note of this: Everyone should be quick to listen, slow to speak and slow to become angry, for man's anger does not bring about the righteous life that God desires" (James 1:19–20).

I don't know about you, but if I'm ever accused of being slow, I hope it's the kind of slow the Book of James is talking about. Slow to speak and slow to become angry. James tells us to have a quick ear, not a quick tongue. Better to look slow and choose to go slow instead of being foolish with unrestrained anger. Seldom is anger the seed that yields the fruit of unconditional love. It's love, not anger, that brings about the transformed life of right living.

Instead of taking your anger out on your spouse, why not try taking your anger to God? God's love can handle it. His love is not easily angered when you're angry and frustrated. God sees the big picture. He sees your perspective, and he wants to offer you another perspective. His. He offers you a

177

more excellent way out of anger, a better way through your brokenness, through the cross of his unconditional love.

His way beats sitting in an anger management class, doesn't it?

By choosing not to become *easily* angered, we can minimize our propensity for keeping a secret scorecard in our back pocket.

CHAPTER FOURTEEN

What Really Counts

When we keep a record of wrongs, when we fail to forgive and forget, could it be that we've forgotten how much we've been forgiven?

Hey, what's that you're hiding behind your back?

A scorecard, huh?

I have lots of scorecards. Golf scorecards. If you add 'em all up, I'd have enough frequent flyer penalty strokes to fly to Asia and back. Might even find some of my lost golf balls along the way. Most of my scorecards are in the low nineties. High eighties on a good day. Best score ever was an eighty-two on a public course in Albuquerque. A definite out-of-body experience. And that was with three three-puts and no mulligans. I like playing at altitude. The ball travels much farther, and I need all the help I can get. But enough of me. What kind of scorecard you got hiding behind your back?

Oh, you've got one of *those* scorecards.

A His and Hers scorecard. They come in all shapes and sizes. Penalty cards. Rules and regulation books. Ledger sheets. Electronic PDAs (Personal Demerit Accounts). You may not be a CPA, but if you're anything like me, you know how to sharpen a pencil and tally up all those marriage mistakes on the long ledger sheet you keep in your back pocket. If we were traffic cops, we could carry a thick citation book to whip out every carbon copy of our spouses' illegal and irresponsible behavior that drives us crazy. If someone doesn't keep law and order in this town, who will?

Our spouses run our reds. They cross our double yellow lines. Flip illegal U-turns against oncoming traffic. Or when they're really ticked off, they even flip us the bird. A serious felony. It's time to take the law into our own hands.

We tighten our chin strap. Pull down our reflective shades. Flip on the lights and sirens. Zoom into traffic. We pull the offending spouse over and slowly walk up to their window.

They're nervous. They know they're in trouble. Third violation in the past week. Says right here in the citation book.

"Excuse me, ma'am. You just left me at home with four kids for three and a half hours to go shopping. You said you'd be back in two. I'll need to see your driver's license and registration."

How thick is your citation book? How many tally marks are on your scorecard? How many yellow or red penalty cards do you carry like a World Cup soccer referee? Every time your spouse says or does something that hurts you, do you pull out your PDA and open your Pocket Quicken to add up all the past infractions?

You do?

Good. Now I don't feel so alone.

Whenever Krista and I are having a good fight, um, difference of opinion, and I pull out my scorecard, it drives Krista crazy. Let bygones be bygones, she says. Drop it. Get over it. What's in the past is in the past.

I can forgive, but forgetting is a little bit more difficult. It's taken a lot of work to keep my long record of wrongs in order. Lots of data entry. Tons of filing. Online backups at www.I'm-never-going-to-let-you-forget-this.com. There's a method to my madness, and now she just wants me to drop it? No way, Jose. If I don't keep a clear and concise record of wrongs, then what are we going to fight about? You want me to stick to the subject and fight about one thing at a time? Boring!

Try as I may, I've discovered that I'm not very good at hiding my scorecard. I always seem to have these verbal slipups. I tip my scorecard and show Krista my hand with words and phrases like . . .

Remember when . . .

The last time you did this . . .

Here we go again . . .

You never listen to me . . .

What's it going to take for you to learn? . . .

Because you did that, I'm going to do this . . .

I don't want to have this conversation again . . .

I know I sound like a broken record, but . . .

Records are those grooved black music disks that spin on what is called a record player, the forebear to what is now called a CD player. When the record has a nick or scratch in it, the needle of the record player gets stuck in the same spot as the record goes round and round playing the same sound over and over again. So say you're playing the Righteous Brothers' hit song on your record player, and it hits a scratch. Sounds something like this . . .

You've lost that loving feeling . . . feeling . . . feeling . . . feeling . . . feeling . . .

> When you and I keep a record of wrongs, we keep replaying the same scratch.

A broken record plays the same music over and over again. But you know what? The music that's being repeated again and again doesn't represent the whole of what's on the record. There are plenty of other songs. There are even boxes of other albums for you to play. The whole record isn't filled with scratches, nicks, and flaws. When you and I keep a record of wrongs, we keep replaying the same scratch. Are you tired of sounding like a broken record? Tired of scorekeeping and keeping your spouse in the penalty box? If you're looking for a more excellent way, here's music to your ears . . .

God doesn't keep score.

He doesn't count.

He keeps no record of wrongs.

Whenever you and I keep a record of wrongs, we're really saying that what counts is our record of wrongs. By focusing on the long list of crimes against humanity committed by our spouses, we are counting the wrong things. Keeping a record of wrongs in the valley sends us on a wild detour that will never lead to the peaks. It is the long way around a problem because we overload our spouses with all the problems we're frustrated or angry about. Progress in a relationship is made one step at a time. One problem at a time. Flash flooding our spouse with a deluge record of wrongs douses any hope of creating a better, more realistic solution. We bypass the straight and narrow road of forgiveness by choosing an eight-lane superhighway that can handle all the backed-up traffic in our heart.

But God knows what counts. Relationship, intimacy, forgiveness, and oneness are what really count. In our brokenness, we are so unlike God, who in the generous display of his unconditional love keeps no record of wrongs. No counting.

We are the ones with calculator hearts and insurance adjuster attitudes. Our husband or wife gives us a little fender bender with an unkind word or broken promise, and boy, are they gonna pay.

We store voluminous data of past hurts, misguided mistakes, frequent faults, and surreptitious sins. We are wired with a fiber-optic line running from our heart to our head. When we need it, we are capable of instant recall. Total recall. We have photographic memories capable of colorful, ever-present emotions that can be warmed up like yesterday's coffee, relived and refelt in a split second. We want justice. We want our pound of flesh. This is what makes the human race an amazing species. Primates just throw dirt clods at one another.

> Keeping a record of wrongs in the valley sends us on a wild detour that will never lead to the peaks.

Keeping a record of wrongs is a serious heart condition. How can we move forward in our journey with a heart condition that's missing a beat or two? Putting another swipe on our scorecards keeps our marriages sitting in the ER waiting room longer than necessary. Call it spiritual arrhythmia. Even a pacemaker won't do. Keeping a close count of our spouses' offenses will forever keep us on the defensive. It will never get us up to the peaks and passes that bring the spectacular viewpoints and inspiring vistas we can't live without in our marriages.

I am so glad God doesn't keep score. If God kept a scorecard on me, I'd have a rap sheet a mile long. If he dealt with me as my sins deserve, I'd be making license plates or picking up trash on the side of the freeway from here to eternity. Or worse, separated from his love forever.

Do you know what God has to say about our blunders and blowups, our slipups and sarcasm, our power trips and oversized egos? When we have a shift in heart that leads us to make a sincere, honest confession of what we said or did wrong, he says we're blessed.

> Blessed is he
>> whose transgressions are forgiven,
>> whose sins are covered.
> Blessed is the man
>> whose sin the LORD does not count against him.
>
> *Psalm 32:1–2*

Transgressor . . . you're forgiven. Sinner . . . you're covered. Pilgrim . . . you're pardoned. Your heavenly Father isn't counting your sin against you, and that means you're blessed.

"Get outta town!" you might say. "You mean to tell me that God keeps no record of my wrongs?"

That's right. I know it doesn't add up, but when you and I confess our sins, they are covered by the blood of Christ. Our countless crimes are covered by the cross. Someone else has picked up the tab for our sin. The coldness of our counting, list-keeping hearts has been covered with the blanket of God's extravagant grace. Like fresh paint on an old wooden fence.

When we receive the free gift of God's forgiveness, our sins are covered in the blood of Christ, who died to keep us from covering up what we couldn't erase, rub out, remove, or sand-

> I know it doesn't add up, but when you and I confess our sins, they are covered by the blood of Christ. Our countless crimes are covered by the cross. Someone else has picked up the tab for our sin.

blast by ourselves. Instead of condemnation, we are called children. Instead of a prison sentence, we're given freedom. Instead of a curse, we receive a calf, a robe, a ring, and an incredible party thrown by our heavenly Father, who welcomes us prodigals home with his extravagant grace.

Wanna hear something even more scandalous? Not only does God *not* count your sins against you, he doesn't even remember them. "I, even I, am he who blots out your transgressions, for my own sake, and remembers your sins no more" (Isa. 43:25).

No matter how hard you may be on yourself, when you ask God's forgiveness, he chooses not to remember what you did in the first place. Oh, I guess he could remember just about anything he wants to remember, but there's something more important to him: you. He knows what counts. Our heavenly Father is a God of relationship, and he desires connection and closeness with you much more than keeping a conditional list of everything you've done wrong since stealing change from the school snack bar in the third grade. (Like I did.)

If you've been tempted to keep a scorecard on your spouse, then you're not alone. If everything in you wants to pull out that broken record and get into the stuck groove of using old hurts against your mate, you're not alone. Even when you know you're resorting to dirty tricks and unfair fighting because what's in the past makes for tantalizing bait in the present conflict, you can go there if you want. Choose the lower road, but know that the lower road is fraught with danger and increasingly bigger obstacles.

But if you want a more excellent way, Paul would say to choose the high road of forgiveness. This is the road that leads to true spiritual freedom and increased satisfaction in marriage. God doesn't count your sin against you, so why count it against your spouse? God doesn't gain anything in his relationship with you by counting your sin against you, so what can you gain in your marriage by playing judge and jury against your husband or wife?

"Well, you don't know my spouse."

I knew you were going to say that. The whole point of releasing someone from their sins is freedom. When you forgive, you are free. When you don't forgive, you get wrapped up in the octopus-like tentacles of the offender's sin. When you freely pardon (not condone or excuse) someone of their sin, you are freeing them to live with the negative consequences of their own choices, just as God allows you the freedom to benefit from the positive consequences of choosing forgiveness. The Bible says that we will each reap what we sow, and when we choose forgiveness, we reap freedom and peace instead of bitterness and the poison of resentment. Someone once said, "When you refuse to forgive someone, it's like drinking a cup of poison and expecting the other person to get sick." I prefer a fresh cup of French roast.

> But if you want a more excellent way, Paul would say to choose the high road of forgiveness. This is the road that leads to true spiritual freedom and increased satisfaction in marriage.

When we keep a record of wrongs, when we fail to forgive and forget, could it be that we've forgotten how much we've been forgiven? Realizing and understanding how much God has forgiven you is the quickest way to cure the odometer on your heart that's adding up the miles of marriage misery. Remember the time you lied? Broke a promise? Failed to follow through like you said you would for the third or fourth time?

Spread a little gossip as if you were only spreading peanut butter and jelly? Ever worship any idols? Okay, so maybe you haven't kneeled before any graven images, but what about worshipping the Almighty Dollar? Or your neighbor's new remodel? Envied a home or two? What about theft? You probably haven't stolen a car or robbed a bank, but have you stolen someone else's praise? Taken all the credit for a minor contribution? I don't know about you, but I'm glad nobody's making a DVD of my mind.

Lest we forget how much we've been forgiven, Paul has a little reminder for us: "For all have sinned and fall short of the glory of God, and are justified freely by his grace through the redemption that came by Christ Jesus" (Rom. 3:23–24). We have all forgotten God. We have all fallen short. We have all sinned. And yet God does not forget us. He frees us, buys us back through the gift of his grace and the redemption that comes from Jesus. Listen to the words of David in Psalm 103:

> For as high as the heavens are above the earth,
> so great is his love for those who fear him;
> as far as the east is from the west,
> so far has he removed our transgressions from us.
> As a father has compassion on his children,
> so the LORD has compassion on those who fear him.
>
> *verses 11–13*

So great is God's love for us that he casts our sins as far as east is to west with no fishing line and hooks attached. No conditions. No counting. No looking back. You want to know why? Because we're his kids. This is what I love about being a child of God. As a father has compassion on his children, so the Lord has compassion on you and me. With the privilege of being a child of God is the amazing condition that he doesn't count our sins against us. He removes everything that's wrong about us and replaces it with a loving relationship with him. A

So here's the most excellent choice before you now for your marriage: Choose to forgive. Love God and love your spouse enough not to count. Throw away the sin-o-meter.

relationship based on truth and grace. A truth that recognizes that though we break God's law and disregard his ways, he still loves us by providing his grace and forgiveness through Christ. This is the new way, the more excellent way, of God's children. It's the most excellent way for married adults who are never too young to live like children of God.

So here's the most excellent choice before you now for your marriage: Choose to forgive. Love God and love your spouse enough not to count. Throw away the sin-o-meter. If your spouse whips that ledger sheet or citation book out of their back pocket when you do something wrong, fiercely love them back with an unconditional love that doesn't keep score. Then have your husband or wife read this chapter.

You see, as children of God, when we count up sins against us, it leads to a counterfeit faith. Our willingness to forgive is evidence of our gratefulness for God's forgiveness. When Paul wrote his second letter to the Corinthians, he must have reviewed his notes on the first letter he wrote. Remember, in Paul's first letter he addressed one sin after another. Wanting the Corinthians to understand the depth of God's love and forgiveness, Paul took the risk of appearing like he had kept a long record of wrongs. Nothing could be farther from the truth. Paul was calling the Corinthian Christians to grow and mature in their understanding of what it means to follow God.

He was calling them out of the old life of sin and into the new life of Christ. He wanted them to understand that not only were they new creations in Christ but also that they had a unique role given to them by God. Let's read some more of Paul's mail and hear what he learned from his own experience with the transforming love of God . . .

"If anyone is in Christ, he is a new creation; the old has gone, the new has come!" (2 Cor. 5:17). God gives you, his child, a whole new way to live.

"All this is from God, who reconciled us to himself through Christ and gave us the ministry of reconciliation" (v. 18). God has balanced our account with him through Christ. We are no longer overdrawn and bankrupt by sin. And we have work to do. Work that isn't always easy. Forgiving one another.

"God was reconciling the world to himself in Christ, not counting men's sins against them. And he has committed to us the message of reconciliation" (v. 19). Christ didn't just take on our sin. He took on the sin of the whole world. I've said it before and I'll say it again: God don't count. This is the good news of Christ we have the privilege of living and sharing. We preach the message of reconciliation by practicing it first in our homes.

"We are therefore Christ's ambassadors, as though God were making his appeal through us" (v. 20). We may not work for the White House or the United Nations, but we do represent the King of Kings, and our calling card is his love. God made him who had no sin to be sin for us, so that in him we might become the righteousness of God. God could have sent a delegate. An angel. Anyone but his own Son. Would you and I send our own son? Our daughter? Any of our children? God sent Jesus, who had no sin, to become sin for you and me so that we could be made right with God.

God wants to show us what really counts. At all costs, he sacrificed the ultimate cost to win us back with his love. He abandoned Christ at the cross to build a bridge of hope over the chasm of our sin and shame, to show us a more excellent way of a love that keeps no record of wrongs.

That's what really counts.

That's all that counts.

CHAPTER FIFTEEN

Nancy Rules

True unconditional love does not and cannot delight in evil or anything else that destroys love. When love rules, marriages grow and thrive.

I have a friend named Bob Munck. He's a recovering addict and one of the most refreshing men I know. Though my family's been operating a mortuary in Southern California for over a hundred years, it's not too often I get to meet a dead man walking. (I'm grateful my dad never brought home his work.) Hearing Bob's story, an amazing tale of God's mercy and grace at work, offers the hope of the transformation and restoration that happen when the captivating love and truth of God clobber someone's heart. Bob's story is no less significant than the transformation Paul went through on his way to Damascus. It is the story of someone wandering down the dark, tempting paths in the valley of this life that are best avoided by staying on the main trail. Bob never got thrown from a horse, but then again, Paul never had to eat out of a dumpster at El Pollo Loco.

When I think of Bob, my imagination wanders all over the Gospels, picturing ruined, ragtag people on the way to meet Jesus. What would it be like watching Jesus heal men and women burdened with every imaginable sin, disease, and disability? Let your mind wander for a moment and imagine these images of miraculous transformation. Can you see the look on the blind man's face when he saw color for the first time? What about the man whose shriveled hand was made strong and whole? Imagine the unspeakable joy he felt when he shook Jesus' hand for the very first time.

When people got around Jesus, he thoroughly messed with the muck in their lives. Fevers broke. Seizures ceased. Bleeding stopped. Sight returned. Sin surrendered. Limbs functioned. Pain ended. Demons fled. Death coughed up swallowed sons and daughters. Wherever Jesus walked, restoration followed.

My friend Bob bumped into Jesus on a binge. In 1974, the Muncks were the typical Southern California family. Bob and Nancy. Three kids. Four-bedroom home. Two cars. Little league baseball and soccer on the weekend. Barbecues at the beach. Bob was a successful financial consultant with a bright future. But doing well allowed him to live a double life. On the outside, the Munck family could have been the poster family for sunny So Cal, but inside, there was a black hole of desire within Bob that seduced him to follow and feed the insatiable god of self-satisfaction. Traveling along the valley of married life, Bob wandered down the paths of alcohol, sex, and drugs.

By the late 1980s, Bob had become what he thought was a hopeless and incurable alcoholic and drug addict. At the bottom of his addictions, he abandoned Nancy and his three sons, Rob, Derrick, and Greg. Soon he was homeless, living on the streets of Santa Ana. He ate three square meals a day: heroin, cocaine, and a quart of vodka followed by a half-eaten burrito chaser dug out of the dumpster in the back of El Pollo Loco.

After a number of years eating out of prodigal son pigs' troughs, sick of himself, sick of his addictions, and just plain sin-sick, Bob got on his knees one night in August 1988 and prayed to ask Jesus Christ into his heart and life. Nobody wanted to be with him, talk to him, or even look at him. Except God. But when Bob came to faith, he was looking for a burning bush ignited by a bolt of lightning, which rarely happens in the valley of our sin and separation. He thought that if God could just zap him, everything would be fine. Gone would be his addictions. His family and financial problems would be solved. No more burritos. He tried God for a few months and found it didn't work. It was back to drugs and half-eaten burritos.

In July of 1989, Bob was arrested for drunk driving in Orange County, which brought him face-to-face with a judge who had issued arrest warrants for two previous drunk-driving cases he'd never shown up in court for. Not exactly the way to win a judge's heart. Bob had seven prior drunk-driving convictions, and with this new arrest, he was granted an all-expenses-paid, three-year vacation to a maximum security jail.

One day, Bob began speaking with a fellow prisoner in the kitchen. The man had seven to ten years of hard time left to serve, but he struck Bob as a person with remarkable peace and composure. The man invited Bob to a Bible study. "Nah," Bob told him, "I've tried that Christian stuff. Didn't work." Over the next couple days, the man repeatedly asked Bob to come to Bible study. He promised to get Bob a seat next to the window, a place where he could look outside and see the trees and sun and sky—life beyond the windowless walls he'd grown accustomed to.

Bob finally relented and soon relished the seat next to the window. He listened to the speaker talk about Paul's letter to the Ephesians, in which Paul describes the free gift of God's grace, which cannot be earned lest anyone boast. After a couple weeks of attending the jail church services, Bob got collared by the Spirit of God. Seventy or so guys were singing worship songs. Bob eyed a silver-haired man singing. He was almost eighty years old. Peace and joy flowed out of the old guy like laughter from a little boy being tickled by his dad. *If this is what Jesus is about,* Bob thought to himself, *then that's what I want.* That day Bob laid down his sword and offered a whole-hearted, unconditional surrender to God. One month later, a judge ruled that Bob had served enough time, and ordered his release from jail. Bob walked through the jail gates a free man, inside and out.

Next came the restoration of his marriage. Nancy had moved two thousand miles away. Had Bob let her, she would have come back out to him right away. But Bob said no. He wanted to make his commitment to God and his sobriety real before tackling their marriage problems.

After two years, five visits, and many long phone calls, Bob and Nancy rekindled their marriage, but under these three conditions. (See, I told you marriage is filled with conditions.) These were three nonnegotiable conditions set by Bob, and I think you'll understand why. Bob told Nancy, "Honey, there's something we need to talk about. For us to get back together, I have to follow God first. He's number one. Number two is my sobriety. I need to be sober so I can follow God. And number three, you're the most treasured person to me on this planet. God's number one. Sobriety's number two. You're three."

No woman likes to be number three. And this didn't go over too well with Nancy. But by the incredible grace and transforming love of God, Bob's actions showed her that he was serious. At first, Bob was scared to death. He'd never followed God consistently. In his own power, he couldn't stay sober or stay true to his wife. He did have the choice, though, to walk by the Spirit, depending on the power of God and the strength of others to help him along the way.

Bob's transformation and the turnaround in his marriage was nothing less than spectacular. Oh, he and Nancy fought and made their mistakes, but both were committed to God's way of unconditional love and forgiveness. Nancy had to get used to the new Bob. Instead of crawling on his knees drunk, he was on his knees praying. Nancy knew him as an addict and liar. Now she had a husband who went to church and AA.

Trust and respect slowly began to rebuild. The Munck family became poster children of God's transforming grace; even Bob's sons and daughters-in-law had given their hearts and lives to Christ, an unfathomable miracle of restorative grace for the whole family.

To meet Bob Munck is to meet a man fully alive. He can tell you story after story of all the amazing transformations he's seen take place in the lives of all the alcoholics and addicts he now helps stay sober. Every day, Bob says, Jesus shows him without fail that he loves him and his family so very, very much. Does the love of God get any more lavish than this?

What do you think would happen if Paul and Bob ever got together to swap war stories about the lavish love of God? Oh, they will meet some day, and what stories they will have to tell. Paul will tell Bob the exact details of what happened on the road to Damascus and what it was like to be blinded for three days with scales on his eyes. Bob'll launch into the story of how his son Greg worked at a Christian summer camp as a counselor and how, one year later, Bob went to the same camp to tell his story of transformation. When Paul sees Bob weep from having the privilege of leading a twelve-year-old camper to Christ, he will barely be able to contain himself.

Paul. Bob. Me. You. Can there be any greater extravagance than going from death to life? Receiving all the lavish blessings of God's unconditional love? To sit with Bob is an adventure in joy. He'll be the first to admit that he's still in recovery, still a sinner saved by grace, but what passion! Bob has a bunch of "Munck-isms" he uses to encourage and help the men he leads in his James 5:19 recovery ministry. A few choice ones . . .

1. "When in doubt, look up to God. He's always there."
2. "When you rationalize, you feed yourself a Ration of Lies."
3. "When I make God my number one priority and sobriety number two, God lets me have everything else. Without God as number one and sobriety as number two, I get nothing!"
4. Denial means: **D**on't **E**ven k**N**ow **I A**m **L**ying.
5. "No matter what happens and how I feel, every day I get up and slug the bag for God. Good, bad, or indifferent, I just slug the bag!"

But my personal favorite is hearing Bob shout at the top of his voice, "Nancy rules!" Bob has learned the simple truth that love does not delight in evil but rejoices with the truth. Bob is now following the rule of love by allowing Nancy to rule. When Bob first got sober, by his own admission, he was blowing it all the time trying to make things right with Nancy. When they got back together and he'd say something unkind or raise his voice, he could now tell that he hurt his wife, whereas before the law of evil had ruled in his heart. Humbling himself, he'd go to Nancy and ask her forgiveness.

Before, Bob delighted in evil, but now he's able to face the truth when he blows it. To Nancy's credit, what made the restoration of their marriage possible is that she doesn't hold a grudge. This is why Nancy rules. Bob now understands that we guys spend the majority of our days conquering peaks and fighting battles. But when Bob comes home to Nancy at night, those tactics won't work in endearing her to him. When he walks in the front door, he shouts, "Nancy rules!"

Bob has found his way of allowing love to rule in his marriage. He rejoices in the truth of Jesus' love for him and the blessing of having his family restored. After years of allowing his addictions to rule, Bob has yielded to the lavish rule of God's love. I know this may sound ominous to some of you reading this, but if you follow the rule of love by allowing your spouse to rule, you may rekindle a deep love in your mate. True unconditional love does not and cannot delight in evil or anything else that destroys love. When love rules, marriages grow and thrive. Our hearts were made to rejoice in the transforming truth of God's unconditional love. We were made to receive and give away love.

> Love does not delight in evil but rejoices with the truth.

Marriage is God's design for a husband and wife to experience the fullness of oneness and intimacy centered in the unconditional nature of God's love. Are you letting love rule, rejoicing in the truth of God's lavish love for you? Is his love overflowing in your life?

When Bob meets with addicts who haven't quite decided yet if they want to give up their addictions, he asks them one simple question: "Do you want to get well?" It's the same question Jesus asked the invalid lying next to the Bethesda pool. Near the Sheep Gate in Jerusalem was a pool surrounded by people with all sorts of ailments and diseases. Lying alongside the pool was a man who had been unable to walk for thirty-eight years. Whenever the healing waters were stirred, everyone else charged in the pool ahead of him, depriving him of the chance to be healed. When Jesus asked the invalid if he wanted to get well, the man's first response wasn't an eager, "Yes! Can you help me?" Instead, the crippled man complained, "I have no one to help me into the pool."

"Get up off your duff! Pick up your mat and walk!" Jesus commanded him. At once, the man stood up, picked up his mat, and put one foot in front of the other. The Jewish leaders cornered the guy and asked him what he was doing carrying his mat on the Sabbath. Oops! Healing and carrying a mat on the Sabbath were definite infractions for Jerusalem's Three Strikes Law. The man said he had no idea who healed him. All he knew was that he hadn't stretched his legs for thirty-eight years and now he was skipping home, humming to "Zippity-Doo-Dah."

The Jewish leaders huddled up and said with one voice, "It's him." They hunted down Jesus in the temple courts, where they got really steamed over Jesus' outrageous claim that God was his Father and that God was in cahoots with everything he did. Jesus said to them, "*I tell you the truth,* whoever hears my word and believes him who sent me has eternal life and will not be condemned; he has crossed over from death to life. *I tell you the truth,* a time is coming and has now come when the dead will hear the voice of the Son of God and those who hear will live" (John 5:24–25, emphasis mine).

I tell you the truth. I tell you the truth. *I tell you the truth.*

Is Jesus trying to get our attention here? Check out Matthew, Mark, Luke, and John—Jesus is more than redundant. Seventy-nine times in the Gospels, Jesus uses these five words again and again: I tell you the truth. In older versions, these verses are translated, "Verily, I say unto you." In other words, Jesus is very, very serious about the truth he is teaching and the truth he wants us to grasp. He wants us to move from death to life. From this sick thing we call conditional love to a healthy, vibrant unconditional love. From delighting in evil to rejoicing with the truth.

Transforming love always flows from the truth of God. Unconditional love comes from God alone, the source of ultimate truth. If we are truthful about our need for God and humbly accept his love, first for our own hearts and then to give to our spouses, then the marriage of truth and love in our lives can lead us into deeper intimacy and oneness with one another. We can only love one another deeply from the heart only if we accept the truth that

God is the source of all life and love. Not us. The great lie, call it the evil embodied in us, is that we are the center and source of all we need for this life. We are not the center or the source. Is it any wonder, then, that husbands and wives experience frustration and conflict when their expectation of experiencing unconditional love goes unmet?

Transforming love always flows from the truth of God. Unconditional love comes from God alone, the source of ultimate truth.

The truth Bob Munck experienced is the same truth Jesus wants you to experience. By listening and following Jesus' words of love, you can cross over from death to life. By God's Spirit inside of you, you can vanquish the reign of evil with the rule of love. The most excellent way of love and the path of eternal life begin not with delighting in evil but rejoicing with the truth. It means listening to the words of Jesus and believing with all of your heart, soul, mind, and strength that he alone holds the words of eternal life. It is following the Spirit's lead to allow love to rule in your life. When you allow the Spirit to work in your heart in this way, by faith you cross over from death to life, from evil to truth, and from conditional love to unconditional love.

So how does this play out in your marriage? Bob and Nancy Munck's story isn't your story. I hope your husband isn't a drug addict. I hope your wife is lying right next to you in bed as you read these words. Your story is different from theirs, but the choice before you is to allow love to rule in your life. It is your choice to choose this first. Don't wait for your spouse to do it. Whether you rule or I rule or Nancy rules, what is most important, in your marriage and mine, is that love rules. And when love rules, we will delight and rejoice in the truth of living and loving in a way that honors God and one another.

So how do we do that? What are ways to practice the rule of God's love that draw us closer to one another? Remember Peter? The guy who denied Jesus three times? The one who walked on water with Jesus? The one who went back to his fishing career after he thought Jesus was through with him? Like Bob and Paul and anyone else who has bumped into Jesus, Peter is a tremendous example of the powerful, transforming nature of God's unconditional love. He would second Paul's words about love not delighting with evil but rejoicing with the truth. To help you and me as we walk through the valley, Peter just might add . . .

> Finally, all of you, live in harmony with one another; be sympathetic, love as brothers, be compassionate and humble. Do not repay evil with evil or insult with insult, but with blessing, because to this you were called so that you may inherit a blessing. For,
>
> "Whoever would love life
>   and see good days
> must keep his tongue from evil
>   and his lips from deceitful speech.
> He must turn from evil and do good;
>   he must seek peace and pursue it.
> For the eyes of the Lord are on the righteous
>   and his ears are attentive to their prayer,
> but the face of the Lord is against those who do evil."
>
> *1 Peter 3:8–12*

Imagine Peter making himself comfortable at your kitchen table. In his hand is a checklist, and like Paul, he's a love guide with a lot of marriage counseling experience. He zips through this simple checklist. "Okay, you two. Here's the game plan: Are you doing everything possible by God's power to live in harmony with one another? Are you keeping in step with the Spirit by being sympathetic instead of sarcastic? Do you practice compassion instead of condemnation? Can you admit when you're wrong? Let's get down to brass tacks here. When you're in a nasty fight, do you both repay evil with evil or insult with insult? Who is most apt to give a blessing first? Who waits for the other person to make the first move? Why?"

Are you keeping in step with the Spirit by being sympathetic instead of sarcastic? Do you practice compassion instead of condemnation? Can you admit when you're wrong?

Peter's a bit intense, isn't he? You both may be squirming in your seats, but there's a lot at stake here. Did anybody say that allowing love to rule was going to be easy?

Peter scans his checklist again. Marks off a couple notches and moves on. "Okay, you both love life, don't you? You want to love life and what God has in store for you. Here's a little secret so many couples miss. . . . If you want to see good things happen in your marriage in the days to come, you must keep your tongue from evil. Let me repeat that: You must keep your tongue from evil and your lips from deceitful speech. You can't love life and love one another with lying lips. If you want to turn from evil and do good to one another by pursuing peace, remember to do it in God's power, not your own. You can't walk on water by keeping your eyes on your problems. Take it from one who knows: You have to keep your eyes on Jesus. And another thing, don't try to go it alone. Lean on God and other couples who can help you out. Mentors. Friends. Pastors. Counselors. Whenever Jesus sent us out, it was always in groups. Remember, there's always strength in numbers."

So what's going to rule in your marriage? The law of evil or the truth of love? And who, following the rule of love, is going to let the other rule? Why chomp on a half-eaten burrito of evil when you can feast on the most excellent way of love?

Just ask Bob Munck. The two cannot compare.

CHAPTER SIXTEEN

The God of Always

God's love is always available. Always unconditional. There are no strings attached. No legalese terms. No counteroffers or contingencies as in a real estate contract. No prenuptial agreements. No awkward or silly stipulations. No doubtful promises. No hmm, let me think about its. No maybes. Or we'll sees.

Planting a garden is good for the soul."

Whoever wrote those words hit pay dirt.

Digging. Sweating. Planting. Watering. It's exactly what I needed as my shovel struck the hard soil from where I stood on a long, small slope in my backyard. My mind was a blur of thoughts. Images, many dark and unsettling, flitted back and forth as I tried to focus on the task before me. The stubborn soil, unrepentant dirt filled with prehistoric clay that is so common along the California coastline, wanted to stay exactly where it was. It didn't want to be pierced. It didn't want to move. Didn't want to give up its settled position. A little like me as I was getting knocked out of my comfort zone.

Motivated by a sea of color I'd seen on a recent visit to the gardens of the San Juan Capistrano Mission, I went into creative destruction mode. At Krista's urging, I ripped out huge bunches of long-stemmed society garlic plants lining the side of our home that leads to the backyard. Pretty in pink but nasty smell, and who needs that much garlic if we're not Italian? We also rid our garden of the evil-rooted, alien-seed asparagus plants planted by the former owner to make my life more difficult. I'm almost positive that when Adam and Eve got kicked out of the Garden of Paradise, their first gardening project was ripping out asparagus roots. Absolutely sinful work.

I now had before me Mexican brush sage, light blue rosemary, pink baby's breath, saffron yellow sage, brilliant cosmos, purple sea lavender, *limonium perezii* to be exact, and a silver-colored plant whose name I don't remember because it was lacking the little white plastic name tag that looks like a tongue depressor. The dusty desert smell and simple beauty of the plants seemed to long for attention, something in them wanting to take root and show off their dazzling display of color. As resistant as the harsh soil was, the damp soft black planting soil incubating the plants wasn't intimidated by its hardened clay cousin. With plenty of sun, water, and fertilizer, the two would eventually get along.

The digging felt good, but turning the earth with my spade brought with it dark thoughts of death, burial, and graves. For most people, digging is about discovery. Searching. Some sort of pursuit. As kids, we dig for treasure. At the beach, we dig for sand crabs or clams. Or we dig to plant flowers or pull up potatoes or carrots in our gardens. But I've always associated digging with death. That's what happens when you grow up with a father who's a funeral director. Digging, to me, is about endings. So as I worked and sweated in my new garden on a beautiful summer afternoon, I thought about the day before, when Krista and I had received a phone call from a close neighbor and family friend of ours informing us that their eight-year-old daughter had been diagnosed with a brain tumor.

Jordi.

One of Ellie's closest friends. With blonde hair and soft smiles, the two of them looked like they could be sisters. Jordi's presence in our family had always been as colorful as the new collection of flowers I was planting. You don't meet many kids you love as your own, but we'd always told Jordi that if she ever wanted to live in our home, that'd be mighty fine with us. Her older sister, Morgan, and Caleb, her younger brother, are also friends and playmates of Janae and Joseph. Get all the kids together, and it's refined chaos.

Earlier this autumn, Ellie and I started a "Dad and Daughter" group with several other dads and daughters in our neighborhood. Ellie. Jordi. Cristina. Sophia. Mary. Just a time to beat around with Dad for a couple hours on a Saturday morning, eating muffins, playing games, singing songs, and making crafts. At our first Dad and Daughter meeting a few months ago, we did a short Bible lesson on finding true treasure in life, because "where your treasure is, is where you'll find your heart." So we then sent the girls out looking for small wooden treasure chests Krista had bought at Michaels for a couple bucks each. Ponytails bobbing, the girls dashed out of the house and into the backyard in search of hidden treasure chests. Once these were discovered, it was time for Dad and Daughter to paint the chests together. And so we sat on the long white benches of our backyard patio table, which was covered with newspaper, so we didn't paint the table purple, pink, blue, green, or yellow. The girls knew exactly what they were doing, while we dads gave color suggestions and artistic design tips. Most of our input was ignored, and rightly so. Put a paintbrush in a child's hand and they know exactly what to do. What eight-year-old girl needs unsolicited advice on painting a treasure box?

Thinking about Jordi and dads and daughters, I heaved another dusty yellow plant in the ground, giving God my own version of unsolicited advice. *God, I am not in favor of this one. Jordi. Cancer. I have no idea if it's malignant or benign. Either way, why?*

As if I get a vote. As if God runs his kingdom by a show of hands.

In the next breath, I'm praying for Jordi's tumor to be zapped to the outer limits of our galaxy. The tumor, we were told by Ray and Virginia, was about the size of a small marble, recessed right above Jordi's tiny pituitary gland. I prayed a vicious prayer for it not to be malignant, though *vicious*, under "normal" circumstances, is not an adjective usually associated with prayer. Call it desperate. Frantic. Pick one that works for you.

When I was younger, whenever I heard that someone had cancer, I never got my definitions right. I always asked, "Now is it *benign* or *malignant* that's the bad one?" I've since fallen back on my college Spanish major to remind me that *mal* is bad, as in any malignant tumor is *muy mal*. *Benign* means you get to live. You get to *be*.

Now normally, I love to plant and work in the garden, to participate in God's creative work by engaging myself in the soil of his creation, but when I hear one of my daughter's best friends has an inoperable tumor parked deep into her brain, the beautiful reflection of life in a bunch of flowers is followed by images of graves and wilted bouquets on tombstones. I'm sorry; that's where my mind goes, oh me of little faith. My prayers and thoughts flipped back and forth from dark to light, from despair to hope, from shadow to a candle flicker. I thought of the flippant words we use in times of personal and national crisis. Do we really know what we're saying when we utter, "Our thoughts and prayers are with you"? I asked God not to send Ray and Virginia all of my thoughts and prayers. They had enough nightmarish ones of their own.

As I thought about death, my mind again wandered to our first Dad and Daughter meeting. Not all the dads and daughters made it to our home that morning, so we had a couple treasure chests left over. One of them became a fish casket. What's a fish casket, you ask? A fish casket is designed to carry the body of a small carnival goldfish after it dies. It is part of the larger carnival goldfish conspiracy that runs through this country, whereby children are taught about life and death situations when they bring home their first goldfish after tossing Ping-Pong balls in glass vases filled with water. The children fall hopelessly in love with "Goldie" and can barely fall asleep as they watch it cruise back and forth in the new fifty-dollar aquarium bought from Petco, the corporate carnival coconspirator.

The next morning, on cue, Goldie is found floating at the top of the fishbowl, and it's back to Petco, where a sales rep sells you a new fish and enough PH water conditioner to alkalize Lake Erie. What Petco doesn't offer, though, is grief counseling. The old Goldie is replaced by the new Goldie, which is part of a larger myth perpetuated in our society that when we experience loss we should replace it instead of grieve for it. And so we replace our losses with food, exercise, workaholism, shopping, drugs or alcohol—anything to distract or numb us from the difficult emotions that come with grief.

I heaved Mexican sage into the fresh hole I had just dug. *Why Jordi and not Ellie?* I asked God. Of course, I didn't want Ellie to contract cancer, but the randomness of the whole situation perplexed me. The girls look alike, play alike, and act silly together, so what microbe entered Jordi's system and not Ellie's? My questions by that time had entered the unreasonable realm, because there's nothing reasonable or emotionally satisfying about trying to figure out cancer, which is why I'm seriously considering going on a steady diet of cigars, steak, and gin. In almost every television program I've ever seen about old people living past a hundred, the secret of their longevity is almost always tied to cigars, steak, or gin. Not once have I ever heard of a vegetarian living past eighty.

I hate cancer.

Cancer has been running rampant in our church. This past year, it seemed like every other week someone on our church staff was either getting cancer or losing a relative to cancer. Including Krista and me. Last March, my sister-in-law's husband, Michael, died after a three and a half year battle with an unpronounceable type of cancer that began in his sinuses. Through the course of his countless treatments and operations, Michael and I had become very close. Michael was handsome. Athletic. A great husband. Loving father of four kids. Authentic follower of the Way. The cancer completely disfigured his face. It consumed one eye and left him blind in the other. During his battle with cancer, Michael became a serious student of what it means to know a love that always protects, always trusts, always hopes, and always perseveres.

Cancer has a way of rearranging life's priorities.

I now have a better understanding of why the Bible says that the body is like a tent. Our bodies are just temporary pup tents with a lifespan of seventy, maybe ninety years, that will be folded up after all our campouts and adventures on this earth are over. The body, though holy and made by God, is a covering for who we really are on the inside. And Michael's outside, his face, was marred beyond belief. On the inside, though, he was still the same Michael we all knew and loved.

> Michael's outside, his face, was marred beyond belief. On the inside, though, he was still the same Michael we all knew and loved.

Yet I can't speak about Michael's body with stoic detachment, as if the physical matter that made up his body was insignificant. When someone dies, we don't just remember their personality and who they were on the inside. We remember the body. We see the face we knew and loved in photographs framed on our walls. We remember Michael's tall, athletic frame. We remember the face of this man we loved—his warm smile, his strong hugs, firm grip, and the sound of his laughter. It's next to impossible to miss the person and not miss the body that came along with it.

It was getting dark as I surveyed the freshly planted slope. I pulled the hose around and soaked my new creation, my thumb regulating the spray coming from the nozzle. I thought about my wife. The news of Jordi's tumor had just about pushed Krista over the edge. Seven weeks earlier, her healthy, tennis-playing mom had suffered a serious stroke, leaving the left side of her body paralyzed. Few guys get to brag that they have the best mother-in-law in the world, and I'm a privileged member of that club. I've always loved Betty's vivacious personality and wonderful laugh. She relishes her role as a professional grandma and is always ready to share a fresh pot of coffee. Krista and her mom and sisters are close, so watching Krista struggle through her mom's illness and slow recovery was just one more storm to weather in a year of heavy gales.

This past year has been a year of perfect storms for the O'Connor family. Times of tears and desperate prayers. A season of funerals and gut-wrenching grief. A surrender of control and a letting go. Wanting hope and feeling nothing but a spiritual funk. Death. Strokes. Tumors. The year wasn't all bad; it did have its highlights. But as I dug in my garden, I could tell my heart was growing hard like the clay soil. I didn't like Michael dying and wasn't in favor of Betty's stroke, and our whole family was now reeling with news of Jordi's tumor. As if marriage and raising kids aren't difficult enough,

209

life presents more struggles and challenges to push even the best of marriages off track.

During these exhausting times when we're up one day and down the next, Krista and I have found that what we need most from God and one another is an *always* kind of love. A love that always protects, always trusts, always hopes, and always perseveres. I need that love from somewhere. From Someone. I wish I could say I was always strong. I wish I could say I'm bulletproof, but I'm not.

As I've written before, my love is anything but an always kind of love. My love is an on-and-off kind of love that is conditional, inconsistent, fickle, and unpredictable, depending on my mood, health, how my week went, or whether the waves were good or not. I'm self-confident, courageous, and inspired at the beginning of the week, and fearful, doubtful, and confused by Friday afternoon. When life becomes difficult, the condition and quality of my love wanes as my emotional resources get drained by whatever crisis is sucking me into its vortex. It's not that I love my wife any less or that she loves me any less. We're just exhausted by the trauma around us.

What has *your* marriage been through in the past year or so? Have the outer circumstances of illness, tragedy, or trauma around you affected the condition of your heart and the condition of your marriage? Or have ongoing conflicts exhausted your marriage? What many couples don't realize is that cumulative trauma and cumulative loss create cumulative grief. One loss upon another upon another has the tendency to bury our hearts before we realize we are suffocating under the weight of deadening emotions. Do you and your husband or wife need to say, "Time out! We need to look at what's been going on in our lives the past year to get some perspective." It only takes one of you to fire a signal flare, and there's no time like today to pay attention to the condition of both of your hearts. Too often, we wait too long to ask for help. And so instead of knowing the signs of when our marriage is in trouble or telling our spouse when we're feeling overwhelmed, we just wait, hoping things will get better. You see, when our hearts are broken, we just don't love as well as we usually do. This is one of the harsh realities of navigating the peaks and valleys of everyday life. I can't pretend it's any other way. And whether you find yourself on a peak or in a valley in your marriage right now, pretending is the one spiritual hazard you want to be sure to avoid.

The moment I begin pretending that my love is better or stronger than it really is, well, that's when the seeds of spiritual hypocrisy begin to take root in my life. One of the greatest, if not the greatest, hindrances to spiritual renewal is pretending. It takes a tremendous amount of emotional and spiritual energy to pretend that we're doing better than we really are. If we pose and pretend, we cannot live authentic Christian lives. Pretending cuts us off from God's unconditional love, because in our best attempts to act stronger than we are, we straight-arm God out of the way. When we are too strong and too resilient for our own good, we miss out on the beatitude blessings promised to us in our spiritual poverty: "Blessed are the poor in spirit, for theirs is the kingdom of heaven. Blessed are those who mourn, for they will be comforted. Blessed are the meek, for they will inherit the earth" (Matt. 5:3–5).

Sometimes we're not even aware of our own pretense. We may be doing and acting as we

> The moment I begin pretending that my love is better or stronger than it really is, well, that's when the seeds of spiritual hypocrisy begin to take root in my life.

always have, but if we are acting as if things are better than they really are and if we believe we can overcome anything with a positive mental attitude, it might be worthwhile to stop for a second and ask, "How is my heart really doing?" You see, too often we confuse sadness with a lack of faith or the crazy notion that God doesn't want us to be sad or depressed. Instead of paying attention to the normal and natural difficult emotions that come with grief, we are often encouraged to slap a spiritual Band-Aid on our broken hearts when well-meaning people spout religious euphemisms like "Don't feel sad. Be happy that your loved one is in heaven. God won't give you more than you can handle." Oh, really?

We hear words like this that seem to sound good, but our hearts don't buy it. More often than not, we pay a heavy price for those who want us to be strong and keep the faith at the cost of our hearts. Tell me, where in the Bible does it say that God won't give me more than I can handle? God allows me far more trials than I could ever handle on my own. When I finally reach the end of my self-reliance, I'm forced to cry out to God, "Okay! You've got my attention. I give up!"

This is when I find my strength.

In our weakness, in our sadness, we find in God what we can't muster on our own. "The LORD is close to the brokenhearted and saves those who are crushed in spirit" (Ps. 34:18). Our pretending keeps us separated from our own hearts and separated from the heart of God, who wants to comfort and restore us. We don't have to pretend when we're hurting, because we have a God who is always with us. A God who always offers his unconditional love and his presence in the midst of our pain. Jesus unmasks our pretense by offering his peace and a realistic assessment of what life on earth is really like. He said, "I have told you these things, so that in me you may have peace. In this world you will have trouble. But take heart! I have overcome the world" (John 16:33).

When I read Scripture and imagine the buzz of village gossip when the Messiah was about to stroll into town, I love the picture of Jesus walking through the dusty villages, dealing with the problems life threw at the people of his day. I love his perspective and I love his response: "Jesus went through all the towns and villages, teaching in their synagogues, preaching the good news of the kingdom and healing every disease and sickness. When he saw the crowds, he had compassion on them, because they were harassed and helpless, like sheep without a shepherd" (Matt. 9:35–36).

In a world filled with cancer, car wrecks, storms, and strokes, we have a loving Shepherd who offers us the good news of God's always love. Have you and I stopped to wonder and gasp that God goes to the ends of the earth to communicate his unconditional love? If that doesn't leave us breathless, you and I need to have our pulses checked. What I love about Christ, the good and compassionate Shepherd who never leaves or forsakes us, is that he is always engaged with this life. He offers us rock-solid hope as we slip and skitter down the steep slopes of our struggles. He doesn't bail out on us when the journey gets tough or when we get weary slogging our way through the valley. When Jesus saw the multitudes who were dealing with all sorts of sicknesses and struggles on their own, he saw harassed and helpless people. People who were looking for someone they could turn to. People who gave up and stopped trying to save themselves. The lepers. The blind. The deaf. The crippled. And like a shepherd caring for his sheep, Jesus entered into the valley of their fears, the pain of their physical struggle, and the discouragement that comes with hopelessness.

Jesus met his people in the valley. Right where they were at. He offered loving protection. Tender trust. Solid hope. Unlimited perseverance.

That is the always nature of God's unconditional love. He's the God of always. God always loves and God's love is for always. Period. God's love is not dependent on our performance. His love is not dependent on our circumstances or problems or predicaments. His love isn't a light switch that's flipped on and off depending on how well we behave or how many Bible verses we've memorized. God's love is always available. Always unconditional. There are no strings attached. No legalese terms. No counteroffers or contingencies as in a real estate contract. No prenuptial agreements. No awkward or silly stipulations. No doubtful promises. No hmm, let me think about its. No maybes. Or we'll sees.

In his letter to the Christians in Rome, Paul wrote:

> Do you think anyone is going to be able to drive a wedge between us and Christ's love for us? There is no way! Not trouble, not hard times, not hatred, not hunger, not homelessness, not bullying threats, not backstabbing, not even the worst sins listed in Scripture. . . . None of this fazes us because Jesus loves us. I'm absolutely convinced that nothing—nothing living or dead, angelic or demonic, today or tomorrow, high or low, thinkable or unthinkable—absolutely *nothing* can get between us and God's love because of the way that Jesus our Master has embraced us.
>
> *Romans 8:35, 37–39 MESSAGE*

That is the always nature of God's unconditional love. He's the God of always. God always loves and God's love is for always. Period. God's love is not dependent on our performance. His love is not dependent on our circumstances or problems or predicaments.

Jesus always promises to be with us. His only condition is that we freely receive his love that we cannot earn or win on our own. And in his promise to be with us, we find that his love always offers protection from life's storms. His love always offers the strength to trust in him and the strength to trust one another. His love always offers the hope that we will get through this valley of death we're traveling through and the hope that we'll make it through together. His love always gives us the perseverance to keep pressing on when we feel like giving up.

In Christ, this is the amazing character and quality of God's love available to us. It is a love rooted in an unconditional promise made to Moses thousands of years ago. "Be strong and courageous . . . for the LORD your God goes with you; he will never leave you nor forsake you" (Deut. 31:6). At the end of the Gospel of Matthew, Jesus reiterated that very promise to a very confused bunch of disciples who, interestingly enough, were filled with nagging doubts before Jesus headed up to heaven. "And surely I am with you always, to the very end of the age" (Matt. 28:20).

Jesus always offers his always kind of love. He offers you and me exactly what we need in our marriages to pursue the kind of love that will get us through hard and trying times. A love that always protects, trusts, hopes, and perseveres is a love that will make your marriage stronger on the inside. It will also give your marriage everything it needs to handle what comes at you from the outside. These are the conditions that make marriages last. These are the conditions your marriage and mine cannot do without. When we choose to receive the always protecting, trusting, hoping, and persevering love of God, we have something to offer the one we love as we make our way through the surrounding muck and mess.

And maybe in the mess, our hearts will soften as we come upon a garden.

Pick a flower.

And find some rest.

CHAPTER SEVENTEEN

Unfailing Love

Marriage is a daily choice to live in messiness. It is choosing to live with failure. Yours, mine, and ours.

Here's a tip for you guys thinking about taking your bride to Italy for a romantic vacation: Stay out of Florence. Go to Rome and marvel at the Sistine Chapel. Venture to Venice and snuggle up on one of those canal boats. Saunter down to Sicily and make manicotti with the mob, but whatever you do, don't go anywhere near Florence.

There's a naked man in Florence.

Women flock to the guy.

When Krista and I got married, we spent a few weeks honeymooning in Europe, but at the time, I had no idea the Italians had a very literal interpretation of honey*mooning* dating all the way back to the Renaissance. Except for missing the train in Paris and having Krista throw up on me on a bus in Spain, we had a wonderful start to our married life (though nowhere in the Terms and Conditions section of our wedding certificate did it say she had the right to throw up on me).

After eating chocolate croissants in Paris and fondue in Zermatt, we boarded a train for a few days in Florence, mooning capital of the world. Florence is the birthplace of opera, but for any guy who thinks he can compete with Michelangelo's superb statue of David, he'll be singing the blues quicker than he can order a café latte. Had I known that I was going up against the bum of a Goliath-sized statue, I would have been more than willing to wear lederhosen and stay yodeling in Switzerland.

After taking pictures on the Ponte Vecchio in Florence, Krista and I strolled over to the Galleria dell'Accademia to see what I thought would be a statue of the famous biblical boy who defeated the Philistine giant. When we walked inside, I saw no innocent shepherd boy. What Krista and I encountered was an eighteen-foot-tall strapping, handsome, and very naked man. Please don't misunderstand me here. I appreciate art, but I would be inclined to say that I appreciate noncompetitive art that leaves no room for junior high locker room comparisons.

"Stop staring," I told Krista as I yanked the camera out of her hands. "And there will be no pictures. If you want pictures of a naked man, take pictures of me, your new husband."

As Krista and the other panting wives in the museum ogled David's perfectly sculptured body, I wandered over to a group of unfinished chunks of stone with whom I had much more in common. Preceding David, the sculptured stud of studs, are four unfinished marble works known as "the Slaves." Michelangelo's inspiration for the Slaves is based on the psychological state of men who have trouble pulling their wives away from the statue of David. *Now these guys,* I thought to myself, *are works of art.* The Slaves are twisted, contorted, half-finished men yearning to break free from their marble bondage. They are ugly. Incomplete. Pockmarked. Unshaven with a course, gritty texture. Straining for the remote that is eternally out of reach. The Slaves are real men.

Standing before David, who looked like a Calvin Klein underwear model sans the underwear, I found I couldn't relate to him at all. Killer of Goliath, now an immortalized lady killer, he stood stone cold, staring off into space. He was aloof. Immune to all the fuss and adoration. *Humph,* I muttered to myself. No wonder Goliath lost his head. Who would want to go into battle against a naked man? Nice butt, though.

The David before me was a poser. Too squeaky clean. Completely unlike the Bible's unedited version of a man who was anything but the lily-white model of perfection standing on a pedestal in Florence. The David you and I know is anything but perfect. Talented? Yes. Fearless in battle? Without a doubt. A warrior poet? The best of his day. A man after God's own heart? The only one mentioned in Scripture.

But perfect?

In the words of Scooby-Doo, "Abso-root-ry not."

David was as unfinished as Adam and as incomplete as Cain. Like most biblical giants, David was anything *but* a model of perfection. His life is a crystal-clear picture of everything we'd like to achieve and everything we don't want to do to mess up our lives. Unless, of course, you like personal train wrecks that drag your loved ones down into the abyss with you.

David's life is a study in contrasts—amazing victories and staggering personal defeats. A holy, loving devotion and a stubborn will that was seduced to sin. A man of pure intentions and wayward passions. Victorious king of Israel and a Bathsheba voyeur. Kind friend and coldhearted killer. Defender of righteousness and uninvolved parent who let sin slide. David enjoyed all the benefits of God's blessing as he hid the law of God in his heart, and he suffered tremendously from the consequences of personal compromise. Swayed by the illusion that a little sin never hurt anyone, David's decision cost him and his family dearly. Nathan prophesied a scathing rebuke from the Lord: The sword David used to kill Uriah would never leave David's house because he despised God and took the wife of Uriah the Hittite to be his own (2 Sam. 12:10). It takes years to establish a good character, but how many seconds to destroy it?

Amazing, isn't it? A man after God's own heart despising the heart of God.

Despite all of his spectacular failures and wild personal wipeouts, David discovered something unbelievable about the unconditional love of God. And this is the point of the whole story: The story of David's life isn't written for us to take notes about his successes or failures. Nor is David's life an executive summary about how to achieve incredible accomplishments while minimizing our risk of personal failure.

The story of David's life isn't so much about David as it is about God. God is the central figure in David's life. But like David, we have a tendency to think our life story is all about us. It's not.

When Nathan the prophet gave David a blistering word from the Lord, exposing David's sin of adultery with Bathsheba and the premeditated murder of her husband, Uriah, David had nowhere to run but into the arms of God with a cathartic confession of his brokenness. His illusions shattered and life exposed, David came clean.

> Have mercy on me, O God,
>   according to your unfailing love;
> according to your great compassion
>   blot out my transgressions.
> Wash away all my iniquity
>   and cleanse me from my sin.
> For I know my transgressions,
>   and my sin is always before me. . . .
> Create in me a pure heart, O God,
>   and renew a steadfast spirit within me.
> Do not cast me from your presence
>   or take your Holy Spirit from me.

219

> Restore to me the joy of your salvation
>   and grant me a willing spirit, to sustain me. . . .
> The sacrifices of God are a broken spirit;
>   a broken and contrite heart,
>   O God, you will not despise.

Psalm 51:1–3, 10–12, 17

What David learned, despite his victories or failures, is that God's unconditional love comes attached with an amazing condition: It never fails. Though David despised God, he was able to say, "A broken and contrite heart, O God, you will not despise." In a later psalm, David writes with humble confidence of God's grace and compassion in regard to his sin and errant ways.

> The LORD is compassionate and gracious,
>   slow to anger, abounding in love.
> He will not always accuse,
>   nor will he harbor his anger forever;
> he does not treat us as our sins deserve
>   or repay us according to our iniquities.

Psalm 103:8–10

We learn from David's mistakes about the unfailing, faithful love of God. We learn the depth of God's forgiveness when we come clean with him. Love never fails, because God, the source of all love, is utterly incapable of failing. Unlike David or you or me, God is perfect, and in his perfection, there is nothing in him that can fail or ever fail in the future. I can't relate to Michelangelo's statue of David and its cool, smooth perfection. I feel much more comfortable standing next to the Slaves, a group of unfinished guys.

Just trying to keep a house clean shatters any illusions we may have about living in a state of perfection. Whether we live in the city or in the suburbs, the country or the beach, the mountains or the desert, our day-to-day life is a constant reminder of just how imperfect we are, which is why we need to remember that life is more unfinished than finished. For instance, right when you think you're on top of things, a couple of starving teenagers come twisting through the kitchen like tornados. This is why perfectionists have trouble becoming well-adjusted parents.

In our search for the perfect life, every so often Krista and I will cruise into a new development and check out the model homes. By the time we leave, Krista's depressed. It's not so much that she's dying for a new home. All she wants to do is pack a small suitcase and live in the model home for a while. Living in a model home would be perfect, wouldn't it? Everything's clean. Organized. Newly decorated. There are no dishes in the sink or toys scattered across the floor. There's a place for everything and everything is in its place. Who wouldn't want to live in a model home?

But that's not reality. Reality is imperfection. Messes. Unfinished chores. Perpetual to-do lists. Our homes are perfect examples of the Second Law of Thermodynamics, which states, "In all energy exchanges, if no energy enters or leaves the system, the potential energy of the state will always be less than that of the initial state." To further illustrate, the Second Law of Thermodynamics works like this: You mop the kitchen floor. You marvel at your finished work in its perfect state. This lasts for approximately ten minutes until one of your kids dispels energy by dropping a gallon of Welch's grape juice on the clean floor. You scream. This dispels more energy, thus creating more disorder—a perfect example of entropy.

Our home dispels more energy than the San Onofre nuclear power plant down the freeway. Krista gets

> Reality is imperfection. Messes. Unfinished chores. Perpetual to-do lists.

overwhelmed with the laundry. I get overwhelmed with the piles on my desk. This weekend it's yard work. Next weekend it's cleaning the garage. There are bills to pay. Letters to write. Phone calls to return. The dust bunnies under my desk are as large as rabbits. We're on the kids to clean up their rooms. Do their chores. Talk nicely to one another. There's wallpaper to rip down and a couple gallons of paint waiting to repaint my office. I need to file a bunch of papers and get rid of old clothes. Just two weeks ago, I finally put up the mirror in Ellie's room that had been leaning against her wall for six years. Good thing Krista doesn't nag.

Our homes, our lives, are so unfinished. So imperfect. Untidy. Messy. Sticky like dried grape juice. Just when we get it clean, it all unravels within a day or two. It's easy to feel like failures, which is exactly why we need God's unfailing love. We need a perfect love to help us put up with all the imperfection around us both inside and out. Our home isn't much different than our hearts. Marriage is a lifelong finishing school for two unfinished works of art. One is called husband. The other is called wife.

Are you in need of God's unfailing love? I know I am. Marriage is my daily proving ground for all my blunders, mistakes, messes, and mishaps. My failures prove my need for a loving God who won't fail me with his love. Without God in my life, I am destined for failure. But when I turn to God, like David, I can receive the grace and mercy available to me through Jesus Christ.

> Marriage is a lifelong finishing school for two unfinished works of art. One is called husband. The other is called wife.

How much disappointment and frustration in marriage is tied to our desire for perfection? How many of us want David the statue, the model of ideal perfection, and not David, the imperfect man with Goliath-sized flaws? Life would be so much easier if we'd have married a statue to park in the corner next to the new couch. We see our spouses' weaknesses, but we want wholeness. We see selfishness, but we want oneness. We see stubborn pride, but we want flexibility. We hear sarcasm, but we want encouragement. We want love, unconditional love, but what we get is strings attached like a yo-yo manufacturer.

And the same is true of our choices and conditions. The standard of perfection we'd like our spouse to live by is the same standard we don't abide by. Imperfection in marriage goes both ways. So in reality it's all about learning to deal with imperfection and unfinished business. Throughout the New Testament, Paul writes of the tremendous freedom we have as men and women, our true spiritual identity in Christ, but Paul is also a realist: We still have to contend with our unfinished and fallen nature. We still have to choose between the sacred and the profane. To love God or despise him. To follow Christ or deny him. And to live with all the gray matter in between.

If you and I have a low tolerance for imperfection, we will be consistently disappointed by our imperfect spouses. The key to living within this frustrating tension is to live by the Spirit and give one another the grace and space to grow in the midst of imperfection. This is a choice we can make that will not fail. In our own power, we cannot love unconditionally, but through the Spirit of God, we have access both to God's love and the power to love in the way he calls us to. Through the grace of God, we have access to a love that never fails. By knowing and experiencing the faithful, unfailing love of God in our own lives, we can learn to forgive our spouses' failures and imperfections as God has forgiven us.

Like today's church, the Corinthian church was a model of imperfection. Just as Nathan blasted David's deception and the concealment of his sin, Paul's first letter to the Corinthians was a scathing indictment to everything they were doing wrong.

223

As Paul continued his thoughts in 1 Corinthians 13, he wrote, "Love never fails. But where there are prophecies, they will cease; where there are tongues, they will be stilled; where there is knowledge, it will pass away. For we know in part and we prophesy in part, but when perfection comes, the imperfect disappears" (vv. 8–10).

Just like the Corinthians needed to hear that love never fails, we need to hear the same good news again and again to overcome our fear of heart failure. When all was said and done, Paul encouraged his friends in Corinth that God's love never fails. There will come a day when nobody will be looking into the future. All that will ultimately matter is the presence of God in the here and now, which will have severe financial implications for the Psychic Hotline. And every tongue will be stilled as we stand speechless in awe of God. Everything we know about this life — our intelligence, knowledge, and understanding of what this world is all about — is all going to pass away. Someday, at the end of the age, when Jesus comes in his perfection, all of our imperfection will disappear. We will be whole. Perfect as he is perfect.

In the meantime, what won't fail us, what won't disappear or cease or pass away, is the incredible, unconditional love of God. True love never fails, and though we fail ourselves, our spouses, our kids, and our friends, we have a love from God that never fails. This is the love that transformed Paul's life. This is the love that restored David back to a vibrant relationship with God. This is the same unfailing love that can transform the hearts of husbands and wives who, like every other married couple on this planet, fail one another with broken promises, hurtful words, and selfish neglect. God's unfailing love is the only love that can get in the middle of a failing marriage and offer the hope of restoration that comes through forgiveness.

Restoration is the promise that follows God's unfailing love. In this life, we don't move from imperfection to perfection.

We move from imperfection to redemption to restoration. The Psalms are David's poetry, his journal of his most intimate thoughts and personal experiences with the restorative, unfailing love of God. In the Psalms, David writes of the life-changing transformation of God's unfailing love. God's unfailing love was so inescapable that David couldn't miss it. It was so consistent with his experience with God that he had to write about it, so we would do well to take to heart what flowed from the heart of David. He writes as one who doesn't have it all together. The position he takes with his pen is not one of perfection but one of a person who is in the process of being restored. Can you hear your heart resonate with the hunger and passion of David's heart for God?

> In this life, we don't move from imperfection to perfection. We move from imperfection to redemption to restoration.

> Turn, O LORD, and deliver me;
>   save me because of your unfailing love.
> > *Psalm 6:4*

> But I trust in your unfailing love;
>   my heart rejoices in your salvation.
> > *Psalm 13:5*

> Many are the woes of the wicked,
>   but the LORD's unfailing love
>   surrounds the man who trusts in him.
> > *Psalm 32:10*

> The LORD loves righteousness and justice;
>   the earth is full of his unfailing love.
> > *Psalm 33:5*

225

But the eyes of the LORD are on those who fear him,
  on those whose hope is in his unfailing love.
Psalm 33:18

May your unfailing love rest upon us, O LORD,
  even as we put our hope in you.
Psalm 33:22

Let the morning bring me word of your unfailing love,
  for I have put my trust in you.
Show me the way I should go,
  for to you I lift up my soul.
Psalm 143:8

I'm sure glad I'm not the only one who wakes up in the morning and says to God, "Show me the way I should go . . ." I'm having a good day if I can get my socks to match. In his unfailing love, God shows us the way we should go as we walk with one another and walk with him through the twists and turns, the alleyways and sidewalks, the freeways and side roads of life here in the valley. And we can't stop. We have to keep moving. We are made to keep moving forward. Closer to him and closer to one another. We're not finished, and we can't stop to stare at statues of perfection in the hope that all our rough edges will be smoothed out without getting some bumps and scrapes along the way.

You and I are not the David in the Galleria dell'Accademia. We are the unfinished sons and daughters of Christ. You and I are unfinished works of art, and our marriages will be masterpieces in the making if we allow God to have his way with us. That's what I love about the New Testament story. The master sculptor is in the daily process of carving you and me into the image of the only one who is perfect. As we allow the Holy Spirit to move in our lives and marriages, God is doing his perfect work of making us more like Jesus.

And when we're tired and discouraged and feeling like failures, we need to remember the words Paul wrote to his friends at the church in Philippi, reminding them of God's unfailing love still at work in their lives: "He who began a good work in you will carry it on to completion until the day of Christ Jesus" (Phil. 1:6).

> Marriage is a daily choice to live in messiness.

Marriage is a daily choice to live in messiness. It is choosing to live with failure. Yours, mine, and ours. It's choosing to live with imperfection just as God chooses to love us with all of our imperfections. This means we have to let go of some of our unrealistic expectations and perfectionism by accepting this messy life for what it really is. Love never fails when two people daily look to God to give them the strength to choose him and choose one another. There's tremendous power in this truth. Power from God to make your own choice and the power of God to make the right choice. There's also amazing freedom that comes when we accept ourselves and one another in all of our unfinishedness. Accept the fact that marriage is filled with failure, but choose to love with the conditions God sets in 1 Corinthians 13. If there are any conditions to live by, these are the ones to pick.

All of our imperfection and all the chaos that comes with it can be a dynamic, creative way to live if we're willing to learn how to love in the midst of the mess. All these power grabs for control and perfection only lead to frustration, disappointment, and ultimately, if we're not careful, despair. What we need is a really wild view of God's unfailing love. If God is willing to show us a more excellent way, then we really can't fail by looking at love from his point of view.

It's far better than gawking at a naked man's behind.

And it just might lead to putting childish conditional ways of loving behind us.

CHAPTER EIGHTEEN

Choosing to Change

Growing in Christ and growing in love is a lifelong process, but the only way we will move from peak to peak through the valleys of life is with an attitude of the heart that celebrates growth and change.

When I was a child, I had a lot in common with Cindy Brady. I wasn't the youngest one in curls, but we were both raised in L.A. smog. We both came from large families. She came from a family of six kids. I'm from a family of seven. Her parents and mine had common names. Mike and Carol. Joe and Jane. Brady and O'Connor are Irish last names. Our parents both drove station wagons with the fake wood on the sides. Both of our dads held the same job for their entire careers. Cindy's dad was an architect. My dad is a funeral director, which made us more like the Addams family than the Bradys. Unfortunately, the Bradys and O'Connors grew up in the seventies, which explains why both of our family photo albums are filled with ugly clothes and bad hairstyles.

Each of our families went on vacations to the Grand Canyon and Hawaii, but I never got lost like Bobby or ate a coral reef for lunch like Greg. When I went surfing, I knew better not to wear a tiki idol bad luck charm.

Cindy and I both appeared on TV when we were kids. She appeared on a quiz show for being a know-it-all, and she absolutely froze like a deer in the headlights. I got my fifteen minutes of fame (actually about five and a half) by appearing on *Romper Room* with Miss Mary Ann, where I skateboarded before all the children Miss Mary Ann could see in her Magic Mirror. You're probably wondering if I ever owned a Kitty Karry-All doll like Cindy, but that's about where our similarities stop. What Cindy Brady and I had most in common, though, were our lisps.

Yes, our lisps. Maybe you remember the episode? I do. I'll never forget when Buddy Henton marched right up to Cindy and began teasing her. "Baby talk, baby talk, it's a wonder you can walk."

"You stop that, Buddy Henton!" Cindy cried.

I was ready to pound Buddy Henton into next week, but I would have gotten into big trouble if I'd put my fist through the TV set. So Peter Brady stepped up to defend Cindy, and Buddy walloped him in the eye. Better him than me. By the time Peter's black eye got better in thirty TV minutes, Cindy and I had become sitcom soul mates. (Don't take me too literally. I was in third grade.)

In elementary school, I was one of the few privileged kids who got pulled out of class every week to work with a speech therapist, which is a terribly cruel word for a kid with a lisp. *Sthpeech stherapistht.* Where was political correctness when I needed it most? Every year from kindergarten to sixth grade, I was ushered out of my classroom, followed by the echoing questions of where Joey was going, and into another classroom with a few other kids who spoke with their tongues hanging out of their mouths like I did.

In my speech class, we all loved Cindy Brady. She was our hero, the TV symbol of our speech defect and the oppression of our disenfranchised existence. Cindy Brady represented the apex of human achievement by landing a major role in America's favorite family television show and overcoming all obstacles for the speech impaired. If she could do it, we could do it. I credit my *Romper Room* appearance to the inspiration gained from her courage and valor.

Actually, I never cared a lick about my lisp. I was the lucky one. Speech class was my ticket out the door. I was given cookies and juice for reciting tongue twisters. I was rewarded with toys whenever I said, "Silly Sally sells seashells down by the seashore." Does school get any better than that? When I returned to class carrying a new toy or candy bar, all my friends would say, "Hey! That's not fair . . . where'd you get that?"

Sthpeech classth.

Year after year, I beat the system. I loved going to speech class. I loved my speech teachers. Why change my lisp when I was rewarded for just showing up? Why change when free cookies, candy, and toys were lavished upon me? My poor speech teachers. I can imagine all the conversations they must have had with my mom, who wondered how I was getting along in speech class. How many times did Mrs. O'Connor hear that her little Joey had to keep practicing his tongue twisters or he'd be speaking like Cindy Brady for the rest of his life? How many late nights did my parents spend talking in bed, worrying if my lisp was affecting my sthelf-estheem and how I'd probably sthpend the restht of my life working at Stheven-eleven?

After seven years of receiving lots of encouragement and affirmation from my speech teachers, I entered my teen years with a very healthy self-image. How many guys in junior high could say that they got to skateboard on *Romper Room*? Why change when I was cashing in?

Even when I became a man, I entered my marriage with no strong need to change my lisp. Krista and I had talked off and on about my lisp for a couple years. For those who knew me, it was no big deal. But since I did a fair amount of public speaking, we thought it might be distracting for people who were afraid I might shower them with spit if they sat in the front row. However, I didn't think much about it until my lisp gene showed up in my daughter Janae. When she hit about two years old and began emulating the eloquent elucidation of her father's lisp, Krista put her foot down. "You go get that thing fixed," she said. (Now my kids watch our wedding video and scream in laughter, "Why's Daddy talking with his tongue sticking out?")

I was actually embarrassed to return to speech therapy. Everyone I knew with any significant problem went to a real therapist, but here I was almost thirty years old and going to a speech therapist. I still spoke like Cindy Brady. The old tapes ran over and over in my head: *Baby talk, baby talk, it's a wonder you can walk.* I wanted to throttle Buddy Henton. I wanted to sue the producers of *The Brady Bunch* for emotional duress for having the gall to ever write the Cindy Brady lisp episode in the first place. Okay, maybe I just didn't want to change.

My first appointment was with an older gentlewoman from South Carolina. I detailed my long history of speech therapy to my therapist as she patiently nodded. She showed me why my tongue hung out of my mouth like that of a cartoon character. We laughed as I asked her a ton of questions about how lisps develop (the plural of *lisp* is very difficult for a lisper to pronounce). I almost balked when she gave me a list of tongue twisters to practice. Silly Sally sucks slimy salamanders. I told her I'd be more than willing to practice my tongue twisters as long as she offered me the motivational tools I needed, like cookies, candy, and toys.

And so I practiced my tongue twisters. I worked on my articulation and tongue placement. I tried to speak without biting my tongue, though biting one's tongue can come in handy and is generally recommended by four out of five marriage therapists. Over and over, I reconditioned a tongue that was quite comfortable lounging between my teeth. I made three more visits to my genteel Southern speech therapist, and within one month, yesth, within one month, my lisp was outta there faster than you can say "toy truck, toy truck, toy truck." And I didn't even get a toy. All that work and I did not receive a single cookie. Not one piece of candy for all my efforts. (Though I just wrote a chapter about not boasting, my speech therapist did say she'd never seen someone lose a lisp as fast as me. What can I say, after thirty years, I'm a fast learner.)

When I was a child, I talked like a child, I thought like a child, I reasoned like a child. When I became a man, I finally put childish ways behind me. I made a change for the better. I lost my lisp. I finally put into practice what I had learned all along. And guess what? I didn't need all the stuff I thought I needed. All the motivational tools and encouragement from others were gone (except for one strong admonition from my wife), and look what happened. I changed. I changed because I made the choice to change.

Fine. Sounds good, you say. But what if my spouse isn't willing to change?

> I changed because I made the choice to change.

I met with a woman the other day who asked me that very question. By all accounts, she was married to a corpse. The county coroner hadn't been called yet, but her marriage was certifiably dead. Her husband was still very much alive, but he didn't want to change. He was dead to the world and dead to her.

I was tempted to take off my pastor's hat. Leave the bum. He's a loser. You didn't marry a man, you married a mama's boy. If you're not happy, why stay?

But then again, I was only hearing one side of the story, wasn't I?

There was a lot of bad advice I could have given this woman. Her husband was stuck in emotional rigor mortis, and she was dying on the inside. Go ahead, I could have counseled, do what's convenient. Whatever's most comfortable. Why wait on God when you can take matters into your own hands? But had I done so, more than a few people might have wandered out of Scripture to tap me on the shoulder: "Hey, Joey, if you think that guy's got rigor mortis and can't change, what about this body of evidence?"

Boy, I would have received an earful from Martha and Mary. Do dead men change? You better believe it. When Jesus arrived on the scene to raise Lazarus from the dead, he told Martha to remove the stone from the grave. "Uh, Lord," Martha said, "this is really going to stink. My brother has been in there for four days." But despite Martha's doubts and Mary's grief over what appeared to be unchangeable conditions, Lazarus defied death and decay when Jesus called him out of the tomb. Impossible change is possible.

On another day, when Jesus was talking to his disciples about making new changes with new wineskins, a ruler approached and knelt before him with this request: "My daughter has just died. But come and put your hand on her, and she will live." Jesus agreed to go, but on the way, someone touched his cloak. He stopped and looked back. It was a woman who'd had a bleeding problem for twelve years. How many times had she felt hopeless, wondering if her condition would ever change? "Take heart, daughter," Jesus said, "your faith has healed you." Incurable conditions are curable.

The ruler was getting antsy at this point. *Let's get going!* he was probably thinking. *The longer the Savior waits, the stiffer my daughter gets*. But Jesus sees death differently than we see death. What's unchangeably dead to us is nothing but sleep to him. When Jesus went to the little girl, he tenderly touched her by the hand, and she got up. Someone who appeared to be dead responded to someone who made the first move. Can you imagine the look on her father's face? Can you imagine the look on your heavenly Father's face when you make the first move in response to his first move toward you?

Oh, and did I forget to mention how Jesus dealt with the demons' flair for the dramatic? I thought I had a speech problem until I read the story about the demon-possessed boy. Demons don't like change any more than we do, though I'm not sure if this demon had a lisp.

A father once came to Jesus. "Listen, you've gotta help me. My boy's been like this since childhood. This evil spirit has robbed him of speech. It throws him on the ground, into fire, and into water to kill him. He foams at the mouth like a rabid beast. He grinds his teeth and has violent convulsions. All this, and my kid hasn't even joined a punk rock band!"

The boy had been like that for years. No one had even bothered placing a bet. By all accounts, there was no possibility of change. Buddy Henton would have had a baby-talking field day with this kid, who was dead to the world and dead to those around him. He was useless. The situation hopeless. A burden to his parents. A steady job at 7-Eleven would have been a glorious upgrade.

Jesus watched the demonic theatrics before him. He was not impressed. Then the boy's father made his final plea: "But if you can do anything, take pity on us and help us."

"'If you can'?" Jesus said.

The man had just used the *if* word. Had God just been dissed? Had the poor father's fear opened the floodgates of doubt and disbelief? Did Jesus raise his eyebrow? Did Jesus smirk or scoff? *If I can do anything?*

No, Jesus didn't mock. Didn't scoff. Didn't wag a finger. Didn't humiliate, lecture, or scold. He looked at the man with compassion and reassured him, "Everything is possible for him who believes." Well, that settled it. Immediately the boy's father exclaimed, "I do believe; help me overcome my unbelief!"

The man was startled. Taken aback. Just like we are when we totter between staying stuck and taking a step toward change. I do believe, God. Just help me overcome my unbelief.

If you and I could only change our character and the conditions in our hearts as easily as we do the simple things in life, how much better might our marriages be? What would our marriages be like if we invested more time in serving our spouses than seeking a better tennis serve? What if home was the first place where you and I practiced impeccable customer service? What if we actually allowed our spouses to give us a quarterly performance review to let us know how we're doing and where we can improve? What if, by the power of God, we actually chose to change? The results could be staggering.

But why change? Isn't it a bit overrated? Do you know any people or couples who think like that? I do. Too many marriages get stuck on a soft sofa of comfort and convenience where one person isn't willing to change unless the other one changes first. Call it La-Z-Boy conditional love. La-Z-Boy love is strikingly characterized by the following unspoken thoughts and feelings: Why change when I'm comfortable letting my spouse carry the load? Why work on my anger when it snaps people to attention? Why be patient when I can nag? Why be kind if she isn't going to be kind to me? Why not be envious when I deserve more? Why be humble when I've worked hard to achieve what I've earned? Why protect my marriage when the wheels are already falling off? Why persevere when the other person isn't even trying?

> Why change when I'm comfortable letting my spouse carry the load? Why work on my anger when it snaps people to attention? Why be patient when I can nag?

La-Z-Boy love. It's a comfortable way to live sitting in front of the tube. Flipping the remote, we channel surf from potato chip commercials to Thigh-Master advertisements, waiting for our spouse to change first. But that's no way to get a marriage in shape. La-Z-Boy love is spiritual lisping. Immature. Not fully developed. A person unwilling to change and grow toward a deeper, more mature love is childish. That's what Paul would say.

Paul understood spiritual immaturity. He'd been a babe in Christ himself. He knew there were plenty of La-Z-Boy Christians in the church at Corinth, and he wanted to show them a better way. As a new creation in Christ, he was done being his former judgmental, self-righteous, Pharisaical self. Paul understood that change wasn't always easy, but he wanted the Corinthians to grow in their understanding of what mature, loving relationships are all about. Paul knew how all the division, infighting, and petty arguments in the Corinthian church could cause it to implode. So, like a father gently urging his small child to take baby steps in the right direction toward him, Paul urged the Corinthians to grow up in their love for God and for one another. Speaking for himself, he modeled to the Corinthians what it meant to have a mature attitude toward growing in love. "When I was a child, I talked like a child, I thought like a child, I reasoned like a child. When I became a man, I put childish ways behind me" (1 Cor. 13:11).

236

Growing in Christ and growing in love is a lifelong process, but the only way we will move from peak to peak through the valleys of life is with an attitude of the heart that celebrates growth and change. Spiritual maturity is not about achieving self-imposed perfection; it's about pressing on. Pressing on toward the life of love Christ has called us to as we allow him to change our hearts. This is the attitude of maturity, a moving beyond the childish ways of conditional love Paul calls us to forsake for a more excellent way.

Not that I have already obtained all this, or have already been made perfect, but I press on to take hold of that for which Christ Jesus took hold of me. Brothers, I do not consider myself yet to have taken hold of it. But one thing I do: Forgetting what is behind and straining toward what is ahead, I press on toward the goal to win the prize for which God has called me heavenward in Christ Jesus.

All of us who are mature should take such a view of things. And if on some point you think differently, that too God will make clear to you.

Philippians 3:12–15

We win when we press on. We win when we persevere. We win when we pursue the ultimate prize, the object of our love, God himself. We win when we choose to change and practice love in our marriage. This is the attitude of love Paul challenges us to strain toward. We will strain, won't we?

For some people, maturing means growing in their understanding of what it means to be a child of God. For others, maturity is taking baby steps of faith with the knowledge they've already received as a child of God. Still others, in order to grow in love, may need to receive divine healing from a former wound that's stunting their growth. For all of us, growing in love and walking in love are not options if we are to bear the name of Christ and desire to see love thrive in our marriages.

Love is the signature of Christ in our hearts. Christ asks us to follow him with a childlike faith, but we are to put childish ways behind us. Paul's implication is clear: However difficult the path may be, true unconditional love is marked by a rugged march toward growth and maturity. To fully become an emotionally mature man or woman, according to Paul, childish ways must be left behind.

To grow in love, walk in love, and be in love, we need to say sayonara to our self-induced center-of-the-universe orientation that wants to pull everyone else into our orbit. That means putting behind us the old conditions that keep us stuck. Our whining. Our complacency. Our suffering servant syndromes. The way we deflect criticism that may, if we stopped to think about it, be construed as constructive. Putting childish ways behind us means being honest.

We need to make the first move and stop playing a game of marriage chess, in which we expect the other person to move first. If you're thinking it's too difficult to make the first move, or if you've already made the first move for the zillionth time, more strength and more love are available to you—from someone who is always making the first move. "This is love: not that we loved God, but that he loved us and sent his Son as an atoning sacrifice for our sins. Dear friends, since God so loved us, we also ought to love one another" (1 John 4:10–11).

God made the first move by loving us with an unconditional love that held no condition over us to make the first move. He is always the one who

> To grow in love, walk in love, and be in love, we need to say sayonara to our self-induced center-of-the-universe orientation that wants to pull everyone else into our orbit.

makes the first move, and no matter how unwilling our hearts may be to change or grow, he keeps making the first move. Since God so loved us, writes John, we ought to love one another.

It takes a childlike faith and trust in God to believe that his love will change our lives and marriages. His love will change you, but the choice is always yours. And let change begin with you. In your heart. Your words. Your thoughts and deeds. You can only take responsibility for your own attitudes and actions. You are not responsible for changing your spouse or motivating your spouse to change. If your husband or wife wants to sit on their duff with a La-Z-Boy love, your choice to love comes with a more difficult dynamic, but you will never go wrong choosing the way of love.

What kinds of changes do we really want to see in our marriages? Healing. Restoration. Renewal. From a conditional love to a change of heart. A husband brought back from his catatonic, conflict-avoiding, uncommunicative state. A wife returning from her wandering ways. A marriage taken off life support because of a divine first move made by God. Do you believe? Yes, Lord, I believe with an exclamation point, but help me in my unbelief.

Changing your heart or your marriage isn't as simple as changing a lisp, but like we've talked about since the very beginning of this book, you don't have to depend on your own willpower to change. From God alone comes the power as you willingly surrender your life to him each day. For me, loving God means allowing God to change me instead of me trying to change Krista. I will utterly fail

> Let change begin with you. In your heart. Your words. Your thoughts and deeds. You can only take responsibility for your own attitudes and actions.

at trying to change my wife, as she will fail in her own efforts to change me. (Except for the lisp part.) From what we've read and discovered so far, God is incredibly more patient, kind, gentle, and forgiving than we could ever hope to be on our own power.

If you think you're on your own, the good news is that you're not. You have a very patient speech teacher who can show you the steps to making the right choices that lead to true change. He looks beyond the impossibility of change, whispers to a sleeping girl, and restores her to her loving father. He casts out destructive spirits that have lounged on La-Z-Boy hearts for far too long. He can show you new ways to articulate your love and recondition a heart filled with old conditions. And you're not without the grace of God to help you make the choice to change. You're not without God's presence to give you the strength to make the first move in the direction of love. God will do his part. But you must do your part. And let your spouse do his or her part. That's the very best you can do.

Your speech teacher is the one who has been calling for you all of your life and who calls you each day the moment you wake up. He is the Teacher who will show you the way. He's asking you to follow his excellent lead. To practice the way of love. To leave childish conditional ways behind. To choose to change and choose to allow him to change your heart. No one can speak to our hearts like he can.

Not even the best sthpeech stherapisthts.

And listening to his voice begins right now by living in the now of love.

CHAPTER NINETEEN

Living in the Now of Love

And now these three remain: faith, hope and love. But the greatest of these is love.

I have a confession to make. I'm a sucker for weddings. There's hardly a wedding I go to where I don't get teary eyed. When I was young and single, though, weddings bored me. Except for the good food and dancing, I was a wedding ceremony clock-watcher. Little appreciation did I have for the words, the vows, the covenant of love binding the hearts and lives of two people. I was an impatient partier. That is, until I got married. And until I had the privilege of marrying other people. Wait, that doesn't sound right. Don't misunderstand that last statement . . . I'm a pastor. The marrying kind.

Nowadays, I can barely get the wedding message words out without choking up. Ask my wife. It's embarrassing, but I'm usually more emotional than the bride and groom. I get a lump in my throat, and my eyes mist up more than a Russian steam room. As I read my marriage ceremony notes, my voice shakes as the bride and groom wonder if I'm going to make it or if they should have gone to Vegas. I'm really quite a mess.

Fortunately, I don't have an emotional breakdown at every wedding. But an occasional ceremony comes along when I'm asked to marry close friends (there's that confusion again). Then I'm lucky to get through it without someone handing me a Costco crate of Kleenex. Like at Chris and Heidi's wedding. Remember Heidi? Our friend with the yak bell?

After driving through the rolling hills and redwoods of Marin County north of San Francisco, Krista and I pulled into the Olema Inn. A former stagecoach stop, the white clapboard inn was built in 1876 and lies in the booming megapolis of Olema: population fifty-five. It's a small bed and breakfast with an outstanding restaurant, beautiful crown molding, oak flooring, and white-painted paneled walls. Classy décor. (I'm starting to sound like a travel-guide writer, aren't I?) A more perfect setting could not be found for a June wedding. And Heidi and Chris's wedding was the epitome of country wedding elegance. Out of all the weddings I've ever been to, this was the perfect Pottery Barn wedding. Clean. Classy. Shabby chic. Flip through the catalog and you'll see what I saw that day. I expected a Martha Stewart film crew to crash the event.

Krista and I had been anticipating this day for a few months now. A great excuse for a weekend getaway to the Bay Area without the kids. Earlier that year, Chris and Heidi had asked me to perform the ceremony for them, and we spent a number of times together for premarital counseling. I'd thoroughly enjoyed getting to know Chris. I appreciated the balance of strength and sensitivity he brought to the relationship. The past few years had been such a long journey for Heidi, and I could now see the light back in her eyes. I reflected on the sweet promise of God in Joel 2:25: "And I will restore or replace for you the years that the locust has eaten" (AMP). Heidi had been through the Mt. Everest of marriage tragedies. Her all-too-personal perfect storm. By the grace of God, here it was, a new day. Her wedding day.

Looking over my notes before the service, I was reminded how fond Jesus is of weddings. I don't think it was by accident that Jesus performed his very first miracle at a wedding feast. How would you like to have been the new bride and groom when the wine ran out at the wedding feast in Cana? How would you like to begin your life together with a major Middle East crisis brewing on your hands? But out of emptiness came six stone jars of fullness. From desperation flowed restoration. Jesus has a way of making a new bride and groom look very good.

Like fine wine, Jesus makes things better in his time. He's busy planning the greatest wedding feast ever, and you're on his guest list. But for now, until the wedding banquet of the Lamb, there is still a lot of life to be lived. Living in the now of love.

When Jesus is invited to the marriage of a man and a woman, he always brings the gift of his unconditional love. The cheap wine of our hurried and impulsive conditional love always pales in comparison with the always flowing wine of his unconditional love. Just when you and I think we have run out of love and have nothing more to give our spouse, Jesus stands ready to fill our cup. It doesn't matter if it's cabernet sauvignon, a Napa Valley chardonnay, or Martinelli's sparkling apple cider, Jesus always saves the best for last. He is prepared to pour into our thirsty hearts everything we need to fulfill our covenant of love. As a gracious guest who takes residence in the hearts of willing individuals, Jesus is the only one I know who transforms marriage messes into miraculous merlots.

Heidi and Chris stood smiling before me. Their family and friends looked on with the hope-filled expectations that accompany such holy moments. As I thought about the goodness of

God in Chris and Heidi's lives, I could barely speak as I read the words, "'For I know the plans I have for you,' declares the LORD, 'plans to prosper you and not to harm you, plans to give you hope and a future. Then you will call upon me and come and pray to me, and I will listen to you. You will seek me and find me when you seek me with all your heart'" (Jer. 29:11–13).

Only God knows his plans for us, doesn't he? So much of marriage is a walk of faith. Through the muck and mess of the valley we live in, we need to keep pressing on to the peaks for the perspective and point of view we've been searching for all along. Read those words of God again and hear them as if he is whispering in your ear right now. *I have plans to prosper you. Plans to help you, not hurt you. I have a hope and a future waiting for you.*

God's point of view, his perspective, is available to you each and every day. His presence is available as you live in the now of his love. But here in the valley, we have to remind ourselves that his perspective is drastically different from ours. The hopes, plans, dreams, and expectations we have for our future are not always in alignment with God's greater plan. If we're really going to be honest with one another, maybe we have to stop and ask ourselves how many of our dreams are really tied to the American Dream. Are we tethered to the cross or tethered to our culture? Do we secretly hope that God's plan reflects the same balance sheet as our financial plan? Will our future be one of bounding from one moun-

> So much of marriage is a walk of faith. Through the muck and mess of the valley we live in, we need to keep pressing on to the peaks for the perspective and point of view we've been searching for all along.

tain peak to the next, living on the thin air of love alone without doing the hard work of living and working and struggling and learning to love in the valleys? How do we follow the lead of God's Spirit to see our lives from his point of view?

You will seek me and find me when you seek me with all your heart.

Heidi's brother, Ryan, rose from his chair and began to read from a passage of Scripture that is now very familiar to you and me. You guessed right . . . the love chapter. Ryan concluded with these final words of Paul: "Now we see but a poor reflection as in a mirror; then we shall see face to face. Now I know in part; then I shall know fully, even as I am fully known. And now these three remain: faith, hope and love. But the greatest of these is love" (1 Cor. 13:12–13).

With these final words on understanding the unconditional nature of God's love, Paul is pointing toward the ultimate hope and future awaiting us in Christ. Paul is directing us toward that final peak—the mountain of God, the kingdom of heaven—awaiting our ascent when the days of our capricious conditional love will be consummated by the eternal embrace of his perfect unconditional love.

Paul picks up a mirror to make his point. But the mirror he holds in his hand is entirely different from your vanity mirror or mine. The Greek mirrors of Paul's day were made not of glass but of a highly polished brass. When you looked into a Corinthian mirror, you saw only a faint reflection of yourself. The result was a less-than-perfect mirror image.

In this life, how we see ourselves and how we see our spouses is imperfect. Flawed and tainted. Not as crystal clear as we would like it to be. But Paul promises that God will finish his promised work of perfection in our lives. We will see as God sees.

I don't know about you, but the more mirrors I have in my home, the more messes I see. If a room is clean, a new mirror is a good thing. It makes the room look larger and more open. In a messy room, though, a mirror just creates more clutter. Joseph and Ellie recently got new full-length sliding mirrors on their closet doors. The mirrors look great, but we doubled the mess in their rooms.

When Paul wrote about mirrors and how we see a poor reflection of what's before us, he pointed to the subtle truth of how we are mirrors to one another. We are mirrors of one another, and we are mirrors to one another. Your husband is a mirror. Your wife is a mirror. Your children are a mirror. Your spouse and children reflect, though imperfectly, who you are. Our mirrors reflect our gifts and our goodness. Our love and our laughter. Our sins and scars. Our conditions and our choices. As mirrors to one another, we reflect who we are, but dimly so. We reflect that which has not been perfected. For now, our perspective is limited. More than a bit misty and unclear.

Now I know in part. Krista would agree wholeheartedly with Paul on this one. Paul says that whether we're on the peak or in the valley, we only know in part because of our imperfect, limited perspective here on earth. We don't know as much as we think we know. Our knowledge of ourselves and our knowledge of one another is limited. Our knowledge of God is finite. Our view and perspective can only go so far. Try as we may as we stand on the peaks, we can't see the vast mountain ranges and valleys and plateaus far in the distance that can only be seen and known by God alone.

Though we think we know each other so well here in the valley, there will come a day when we will fully know ourselves and one another just as we are fully known by God. In heaven, you will get to see yourself as you really are. You will see your spouse as he or she really is. All the imperfections and character flaws will be removed. Cellulite and wrinkles included. Won't that be nice? And you will stand before your Creator to see him in all his majesty and glory. You shall know fully as you are fully known.

So what now? Until that day when all the hassles and hardships, the victories and defeats, the successes and failures of this life are over, what do we do with our lives and our marriages?

We live in the now.

The now of faith, hope, and love.

Marriage is all about being anchored in the here and now of faith, hope, and love. Forget about yesterday. It's over. Gone. Finished. Leave the future up to God. That's his domain, and he's the CEO of the universe, not you. Your job . . . my job is to remain. Abide. Stay. To live in the now of love. You and I can't access the unconditional love of God yesterday, and we can't force our way into the future. The wounds and hurts of the past are only healed in the present. The fear and anxiety of the future can only be declawed by a courageous commitment to live in the unconditional love of God today.

The message to remain, stay, and abide in the unconditional love of God is the Holy Spirit whispering to you through the echoes of the centuries. As we slog and plod on the trail before us, our true companion, comforter, and friend, the Holy Spirit, nudges us to remember the words of Jesus: "I have told you these things, so that in me you may have peace. In this world you will have trouble. But take heart! I have overcome the world" (John 16:33). From having our hearts anchored in the now of faith, hope, and the unconditional love of Jesus, we will find the peace our hearts desire.

> Marriage is all about being anchored in the here and now of faith, hope, and love.

Remaining in the unconditional love of God begins with choosing to receive what is freely given. You can only

> You can only give unconditional love without all of your terms and conditions by first receiving it from God.

give unconditional love without all of your terms and conditions by first receiving it from God. Without having your heart anchored in God's love, your marriage cannot climb to the peaks. Without the anchors of faith, hope, and love, you may skirt around the foothills, but you will never stand at the highest summit to receive the perspective and direction your marriage needs to travel through the valleys below.

Early in my marriage, I was an avid rock climber. Krista and I even got a climbing rope for a wedding gift. Now I'm just a jungle gym for my kids to climb on, but I still know the importance of setting anchors in my life. Ask any climber and they will tell you that you have no business being on any climbing route without a thorough knowledge of how to set anchors. Whether you're twenty feet off the deck or dangling two thousand feet off a granite wall waiting to climb your next pitch, your life and the lives of others depend on knowing how to set firm and solid anchors.

Remember the Everest climbing expedition I wrote about in the introduction? One of the key mistakes made that day was the delay in setting the fixed ropes and anchors on the Hillary Step. It took the climbers far too long to set their anchors in order to make their way to the top. Climbing historians will debate the issues, but one of the contributing factors to the resulting tragedy was that the climbers waited for *someone else* to set the anchors first. They waited for *someone else* to make the first move. A delay or lack of knowledge of how to set anchors only leads to tragedy.

A number of years ago when I was a youth pastor, two former students of my youth group went rock climbing in Joshua

Tree National Monument. The route they chose to climb was moderately difficult. Together, they had bagged tougher routes. This one was definitely within their ability levels. In their climbing guidebook, the map of the route showed a fixed piton near the top on the route. An anchor. A fixed piece of protection to clip into with a carabiner and a rope. One guy led the climb. The other belayed. After setting a couple anchors and climbing past a portion of the rock where he couldn't be seen by his belayer, the lead climber yelled down to his buddy that he couldn't locate the anchor that was shown on the map. He was already dangerously above his last anchor, some eight to twelve feet above. He yelled again that he couldn't find a good place to secure a new anchor. In a very short period of time, he lost his grip and fell to his death. There was no fixed piton. No anchor. No nothing.

How many of us are still flipping through the old guidebooks of conditional love? How many of us are climbing up the route of a self-seeking love that we have no business being on? How many of us are leaving the here and now anchors of faith, hope, and love for paths that will never lead us to the peaks? Isn't it time to renew our thoughts, attitudes, habits, and behaviors with the most reliable Guidebook, which promises to show us the most excellent way to live? Are we waiting for someone else to set the anchors of faith, hope, and love in our lives? Are we waiting for someone else to make the first move? Are we so busy searching for an easier way that we forget that the most excellent way is right before us in the here and now?

Choosing the most excellent way of God's unconditional love won't prevent the stormy weather conditions on the road ahead, but it will transform the spiritual condition of your heart and how you weather the inevitable storms of life. With the Holy Spirit as the best Guide you could ever have, these three anchors will help you stand through the strongest of storms. You and I can't get away from the messes in the valley, but we can choose to walk in God's Spirit, allowing him to anchor us in faith, hope, and love in the here and now.

A marriage is nothing less than the Song of Solomon pursuit of a lover after his beloved. It is the celebration of a man and woman pursuing the transformational path of unconditional love that brings joy and laughter to the heart of God. You are the beloved of God, and it is the anchors of faith, hope, and love that lash you to his grace. This is what God makes available to you: A true marriage spirituality rooted in him, anchored in the here and now of faith, hope, and love. You are not alone. You are not without a Guide. You are not without a Guidebook. The anchors are all yours just for the asking. Putting aside all the conditions of conditional love, you can have and experience the transforming unconditional love of God on one condition. It's the same thing I've been saying all along: God loves you unconditionally . . . on one condition. Accept the free gift of his love in the here and now.

And so we press on in the valley. We will always yearn for the clear perspective we find on the peaks, but God's perspective is available to you and me every day here in the valley. Remember, you and I can't live on the thin air of love alone. The valley is where the oxygen is thick and plentiful. The valley is where we learn to love and connect and belong. The valley is where we are reminded of God's lavish love and rediscover that there is meaning in the mess.

> Choosing the most excellent way of God's unconditional love won't prevent the stormy weather conditions on the road ahead, but it will transform the spiritual condition of your heart and how you weather the inevitable storms of life.

Let me say that again: There is meaning in the mess. The muck and mess is where we live, work, and play. That includes the mess in the kitchen. The unpaid bills. The traffic tickets and terrible customer service. The mess is a sign of life, and God makes his three anchors of faith, hope, and love available to you just for the asking.

> You are the beloved of God, and it is the anchors of faith, hope, and love that lash you to his grace.

Oh, we see so faintly the real life all around us in the here and now of God's gracious love. The brilliant radiance of pink cosmos. The sweet summer smell of suntan lotion on our children's faces. The pleasure of going out for a good meal with friends. The glow of a candlelight anniversary dinner. Prayers at bedtime. All the scraped knees, Bactine, and Band-Aids. Carrying a sleeping three-year-old out of the theater at the end of a Disney movie. Bursting with dive-hood laughter and wrestling our kids into sweaty exhaustion. Sweet-pea picking and putting up with prima donnas. Pottery Barn weddings and a bride's bouquet. Renewal and restoration. Holy moments. All of these. We live and breathe and move through the paradox of pressing forward in the valley while staying in the now of faith, hope, and love. Right now, let these words sink deep into your heart. Now abide. Now stay. Now remain. In faith. In hope. In love.

And the greatest of these is love.

Live in the now of his love.

Notes

1. Michael Yaconelli, *Messy Spirituality* (Grand Rapids: Zondervan, 2002), 96.

2. William Barclay, *The Letters to the Corinthains,* rev. ed. (Philadelphia: Westminster Press, 1975).

3. Thomas Merton, *No Man Is an Island* (Orlando: Harcourt Brace, 1955), xxi.

4. St. John of the Cross, quoted in David Hazard, *You Set My Spirit Free* (Minneapolis: Bethany, 1994), 30–31.

5. From *The Concise Matthew Henry Commentary on the Bible.* Found on Christianitytoday.com.

6. Jan Johnson, "Walking with God through Frustration," *Weavings* 41 (July/August 2003): 33.

Joey O'Connor is the author of fifteen books for couples, parents, and young adults. He serves as a pastor at Coast Hills Community Church in Aliso Viejo, California. He is also the founder and executive director of the Grove Center for the Arts, a ministry dedicated to nurturing the spiritual development and creative vision of artists in the church. Joey, his wife, Krista, and their four children live in San Clemente, California, and in a pup tent somewhere near the Southwest border.

You can reach Joey at his web site: www.joeyo.com

For more information about the Grove Center for the Arts, you can reach us at www.thegrovecenter.org or call (949) 369-6767.